MANAGING THE
INVESTIGATIVE UNIT

ABOUT THE AUTHOR

Daniel S. McDevitt, completed a thirty-six-year law enforcement career, which began with his appointment as a Special Agent with the Naval Criminal Investigative Service (NCIS). He then served for 24 years with the Illinois State Police (ISP), retiring as a Captain, and subsequently served for ten years as Chief of Police in two Chicago suburbs.

McDevitt has a Master of Science degree in Criminology, is a graduate of the FBI National Academy and the FBI Executive Development Program, and has taught at colleges, universities, and police academies in the United States, Europe, Africa, Asia, and the Middle East for both civilian and military law enforcement personnel. He has authored three books: *Police Chief-Attaining and Succeeding in this Critical Position, Major Case Management-A Guide for the Law Enforcement Manager,* and *Managing the Investigative Unit,* and several law enforcement and management articles, and has served as a consultant for both governmental agencies and private corporations.

He is also retired as an Intelligence Officer with the U.S. Navy, where he held the rank of Lieutenant Commander after completing a twenty-year career which included both enlisted and commissioned service, As a Medical Corpsman he cared for Vietnam wounded personnel, and later as an Intelligence Officer, he specialized in foreign counterintelligence and analysis of terrorist operations. He was recalled to active duty for the Gulf War, where he conducted countersurveillance operations and protective services.

McDevitt has served as a consultant for the U.S. Department of State on several occasions, and has developed and presented courses internationally for the State Department's Anti-Terrorism Assistance Program and for the Department of Defense Executive Institute throughout Africa, Asia, the Middle East, and Europe. He has also planned and conducted dignitary protection details for high-profile individuals

He is the co-owner of REM Management Services, Inc., a management consulting firm. The firm provides a variety of public safety, security, and management services and training programs for corporate, business, and government clients worldwide.

McDevitt and his wife Marilyn have been married since 1972 and have two children and four grandchildren.

Second Edition

MANAGING THE INVESTIGATIVE UNIT

By

DANIEL S. McDEVITT, B.S., M.S.

Chief of Police (Retired)
Lansing, Illinois Police Department
Captain, Illinois State Police (Retired)

CHARLES C THOMAS · PUBLISHER, LTD.
Springfield · Illinois · U.S.A.

Published and Distributed Throughout the World by

CHARLES C THOMAS • PUBLISHER, LTD.
2600 South First Street
Springfield, Illinois 62704

©2012 by CHARLES C THOMAS • PUBLISHER, LTD.

ISBN 978-0-398-08809-5 (hard)
ISBN 978-0-398-08810-1 (paper)
ISBN 978-0-398-08811-8 (ebook)

Library of Congress Catalog Card Number: 2012008003
First Edition, 2005
Second Edition, 2012

With THOMAS BOOKS *careful attention is given to all details of manufacturing
and design. It is the Publisher's desire to present books that are satisfactory as to their
physical qualities and artistic possibilities and appropriate for their particular use.*
THOMAS BOOKS *will be true to those laws of quality that assure a good name
and good will.*

Printed in the United States of America
CR-R-3

Library of Congress Cataloging-in-Publication Data

McDevitt, Daniel S.
  Managing the investigative unit / by Daniel S. McDevitt. -- 2nd ed.
    p. cm.
  Includes index.
  ISBN 978-0-398-08809-5 (hard) -- ISBN 978-0-398-08810-1 (pbk.) -
- ISBN 978-0-398-08811-8 (ebook) 1. Criminal investigation. 2. Crime
scene searches. 3. Police training. I. Title.

  HV8073.M333 2012
  363.25068–dc23

                                                    2012008003

PREFACE

The purpose of this book is to provide you, the investigative manager, with some of the tools and techniques necessary to successfully manage the investigative unit. Hopefully this is more than merely an exercise in the theoretical, as you will also be provided with several procedures and forms that can be adapted for your own agency. Before we get to those, however, you must understand the mindset of the police investigator. Investigators are very different from patrol officers, and this must be remembered when managing them or the process will not go smoothly.

Investigators, regardless of the size of the agency, seem to have some common traits:

1. They decide who gets to be one of them, regardless of who gets assigned to the unit by the department. Investigators have very strict mechanisms for entering their little corner of the world. Only the chosen few are allowed into their ranks, and acceptance by fellow investigators is not automatically granted.
2. Investigators have an esoteric knowledge (a sixth sense?) that goes beyond technical expertise and usually beyond that of patrol officers. Although all experienced cops have this esoteric knowledge to some degree, this knowledge and ability is honed to its sharpest form in the investigator.
3. Whereas all police officers have internal sanctions to govern their own, both of the formal and the informal variety, investigators have raised this concept to an art form. To watch a group of investigators apply their own sanctions to a fellow investigator who isn't carrying his or her own weight or who commits some other transgression is truly an interesting phenomenon.

In order to be an effective manager of investigators, you must recognize these traits and be prepared to address investigators who sometimes have a tendency to go overboard on any of them. This is particularly true for the newly assigned supervisor who has either no experience in an investigative assignment or a very limited investigative background. Many law enforcement agencies seem to believe that good managers can effectively manage anybody and try to prove their theory by cross-assigning patrol and investigative supervisory and management personnel, sometimes for no apparent reason. Too often, this can lead to heartache, headache, and ultimate failure for the cross-assigned supervisor or manager. There are many common threads to successful management, but assigning someone to manage an investigative unit with little or no investigative background often ends in disaster, poor morale, and poorly conducted investigations.

The role of the investigator is without question the most glamorous in the PD. Movies and television programs about police demonstrate that the majority are about investigators instead of patrol officers. The reason is that the job of the investigator just *seems* to be more interesting and somehow sexier than the role of the patrol officer.

The investigator is portrayed in movies, books, and TV as a meticulous and tireless gatherer of evidence that always leads to the arrest and conviction of the criminal. Another one of my favorite definitions of an investigator is "a super cop, who is a bit unorthodox, normally at odds with his superiors, and willing to bend the rules, he is embedded in a web of unsavory informants, still always able to keep his integrity in his unrelenting pursuit of crime and the master criminal." Whenever I hear this one, I imagine the theme from the 1950s series *Superman* playing in the background with an investigator standing in front of an American flag wearing a cape (of course) blowing in the breeze. Unfortunately, a lot of the public, and even some patrol officers, believe this nonsense.

In order to effectively manage investigators, you must first consider what it is that investigators *actually do every day*–that is to say, the role of the investigator. The true role of the investigator is basically found in what I call the "shoe leather" approach to solving crimes. In reality, the role of the investigator is not glamorous at all. What investigators actually do is to complete (and sometimes repeat) a series of methodical, plodding, and often very boring tasks. Hours and hours of (often seemingly pointless) surveillances and countless interviews are the routine, not the exception. The investigator spends a great deal of time making endless (and sometimes frustrating) attempts to control uncontrollable witnesses, some of whom need constant placating or even babysitting. The investigator spends long periods of time preparing very detailed reports that the defense counsel will use every trick at their disposal to decimate in court. Unlike most patrol personnel, the investigator's schedule is not confined to an 8-hour-a-day shift. To the contrary, call-outs, extra hours, and missed holidays, family gatherings, and other social events are the rule rather than the exception.

Some would say the real difference between patrol officers and investigators is that patrol officers merely *think* that they know everything whereas investigators, on the other hand, are *absolutely certain* that they know everything and equally as certain that patrol officers know nothing. Although that's meant to be humorous, most investigative unit managers with whom I am familiar would agree that there is a little ring of truth hiding in that sarcasm.

Managing the investigative unit can be an extremely rewarding part of any law enforcement professional's career, or it can be an absolute nightmare. The strategies and techniques you will read about in this book will help make the experience rewarding. It is worth noting that many of these techniques and strategies were learned through the "school of hard knocks," and many are the direct result of ideas that failed miserably. Rather than force you to learn some of these lessons the hard way as I did, this book is designed to help you develop the skills you need to hit the ground running and successfully manage your agency's investigative unit.

D.S.M.

ACKNOWLEDGMENTS

Since this book was first published in 2005, a number of changes have occurred in my life. I ended my 36-year law enforcement career in 2009, and took the management consulting firm that a police partner of mine and I had started years earlier and worked it into a full-time undertaking. I had a great law enforcement career, and miss a lot since it has ended. Most of all, I miss the great men and women with whom I worked.

I've expanded my teaching to the international level, developing and presenting courses for the State Department's Anti-Terrorism Assistance Program and the Defense Department Counter-Trafficking Executive Institute. These programs have taken me to Kenya, Jordan, Mali, Algeria, Kazakhstan, and Afghanistan. All this travel has resulted in my having the privilege to meet, instruct, and work with cops from all over the world. Those experiences have confirmed in my mind what I've always believed to be true—we cops are all the same. We came into our profession for the same reasons, have the same goals of safety, security, and justice for our communities, and want to "do the right thing." We take our profession very seriously, and care sincerely for those we serve.

I've had changes in my personal life as well, I've had two additional books published *Major Case Management* and *Police Chief-How to Attain and Succeed at this Critical Position,* and several articles. My wife Marilyn and I now have four grandchildren, Kylie, Olivia, Tanner Daniel, and Liam Daniel. Life is good.

CONTENTS

MANAGING THE
INVESTIGATIVE UNIT

Chapter 1

HOW DID YOU GET HERE?

Perhaps the biggest factor that will impact the ease with which the new investigative manager fits into their new role is how they got to the position in the first place.

There are basically two ways in which people are assigned as managers of investigative units. I call these *Home Grown* and *Out of Left Field*. In the Home Grown situation, the person assigned as the new investigative manager is either currently an investigator who has been promoted into the manager's position, or has been an investigator at some point in their career.

The "Out of Left Field" situation involves someone being assigned as an investigative manager who has no background whatsoever in an investigative position.

Many agencies, particularly in times of economic uncertainty, (which seems to be the rule rather than the exception) sometimes takes the "one size fits all" approach to the assignment of management personnel. While this would appear in theory to be a very "fiscally responsible" method of assigning personnel, it oftentimes doesn't work in actual practice. This approach to management is based on the premise that a good manager can manage any unit or element to which they are assigned in the organization. While it is true that some of the elements of good management are constant, there are subtle (and sometimes not so subtle) nuances to various units or elements of organizations that should not be overlooked. Simply putting someone into a management position and hoping that they will learn whatever they need to know about the position, the personnel, and the tasks being accomplished is really an overly optimistic view of management.

3

We've all heard of the "Peter Principle," where someone rises to their own level of competence and then gets promoted one step above that. In many instances, that is exactly what some police departments do when they take someone who is totally competent at one assignment and arbitrarily assign them to something completely different, and something for which they have no preparation. This often makes the newly assigned manager appear to be a living, breathing example of the Peter Principle, which is usually not the case.

The investigative manager who has a "Home Grown" background has several advantages when taking over an investigative unit, which include:

- **Familiarization with how investigations are conducted**- there is no substitute for having actually conducted investigations from start to finish. Someone in an investigative management position who has never done this is at a distinct disadvantage, and should spend some time familiarizing themselves with the manner in which different types of investigations are conducted. This can be accomplished by taking classes on criminal investigations, studying agency case reports, and discussing cases with their predecessor in the investigative unit as well as with the investigators themselves.
- **Familiarity with investigator's methods**- It would seem obvious that in a criminal investigation that the investigator would go from "Step A" to "Step B" and so on, but with criminal investigations that isn't always the case. As a matter of fact, criminal investigations that go strictly according to an investigative plan and in perfect order are definitely the exception rather than the rule. When working narcotics enforcement units we had a saying that "if one out of five drug deals go according to plan, we're doing great."

In most investigations, the investigators conducting them must be flexible enough to see that there are situations in which they will have to vary the sequence of events, eliminate some steps, or go in a completely different direction. Personnel who have conducted investigations deal with this on a daily basis and fully realize that it is something that can't be avoided, but people who've never conducted an investigation might find this somewhat strange.

- **Ability to prioritize assignments**- some investigations or investigative steps must be completed as soon as possible, some others when you get a chance, and some can be ignored until much later in the case, perhaps even delayed until case closing. Investigators know this, almost instinctively, and they usually make the correct priority decisions. Someone with no real investigative background might have a difficult time trying to prioritize these decisions, which could be detrimental to the investigation being conducted.
- **Most importantly, credibility with subordinates**- the "Home Grown" investigative manager has "been there and done that," and the personnel that he or she is supervising will usually recognize that fact. The level of credibility that a subordinate attributes to a supervisor is critical, and can have a tremendous impact, not only on the relationship between them, but on the method in which they will accept supervisory input, in the amount of effort that the subordinate is willing to expend, and in the overall morale of the unit.

Credibility is a critical part of any manager's position, and investigative managers who begin a new assignment without the benefit of credibility with their subordinates have a very difficult way to go.

When personnel perceive their manager to have credibility, they're much more likely:

- **Be proud to be a part of an organization or unit** - this feeling of "inclusion" and unit cohesiveness can be critical in the investigative assignment. The long hours and sometimes very frustrating nature of investigative work is made much more difficult in units in which personnel assigned have no personal pride in their unit or organization.
- **Feel a strong sense of "team spirit"** - which is very important. Perhaps the most cohesive unit to which I was ever assigned included a very "eclectic" group of individuals. Some of the personnel assigned had extensive investigative background, some had extremely limited backgrounds. Some of the personnel had an outstanding work ethic, while others could legitimately be considered "marginal performers" (which will be discussed in Chapter 12). Through it all, and even considering our many differences, the personnel in the unit meshed extremely well and the unit was

very successful. I attribute a great deal of that to the credibility possessed by the group's leader. He was an outstanding leader who possessed a wealth of experience, but who wasn't averse to allowing us to "spread our wings" and manage our own cases.

- **See their personal goals as consistent with those of the unit or organization** - in the event that the personal goals of the investigative unit members are either contrary or "out of kilter" with the overall goals of the unit, chaos can ensue. Investigative efforts will not be properly focused, and the attention to detail will suffer. The goals of investigative personnel must be consistent with those of the unit or organization as it relates to prioritization of investigative assignments and the method in which cases are managed, or investigative continuity will surely suffer.

- **Feel attached and committed to the unit or organization**- when thinking about the cohesive unit I mentioned earlier, I can remember several times when we would work all day, chasing down leads, going to court, and writing reports. We would then change gears for the evening hours during which we would conduct our undercover operations, such as purchase of stolen property, surveillances, or whatever we happened to be doing at the time. Particularly on nights when we'd make a good arrest, we'd all go out for pizza and beer after the operations. Ending up our day, sometimes in the "wee hours", we'd have to decide who was going to transport our prisoners to their "bond hearings" the next morning. Even though everyone had worked all day and most of the evening, we never had to be ordered to get up early the next morning to transport prisoners. It didn't matter whose case it was, or who would be filing the charges, the fact was that *our squad* had made the arrest, so we all jumped in to help. As a manager of many units in the years since then, I always remember the days in that assignment fondly and have always strived to duplicate that level of commitment among my own subordinates.

The investigative manager who has an "Out of Left Field" background is placed into one of the most difficult situations for any manager. The person in this position begins the assignment with several disadvantages, which include:

- **No real knowledge of how investigations are conducted**- while most police supervisors, or anyone with a TV set, have at least some idea of the method in which investigations are conducted, that knowledge is sometimes very superficial. Never having conducted a complete investigation does put this type of investigative manager at a definite disadvantage. The fact that on TV all cases are solved in an hour, and the fact that the Crime Scene Investigator (CSI) can instantly deduce not only the identity, but also the whereabouts, shoe size, and parental lineage of a suspect from a single strand of hair can give someone with no real knowledge of investigations some very unrealistic expectations of what investigators are actually capable of doing.

• **No real knowledge of the methods used by investigators**-similar to the "substitute teacher" in junior high school who can be convinced of almost anything by some of the more "imaginative" students, the investigative manager who has no investigative background can be easily taken advantage of or sometime even "conned" by the more "imaginative" investigators as they have no real knowledge of the methods or procedures common to investigators. This has led to some serious problems for some investigative managers, and I am personally familiar with some of these situations.

In one case I was speaking with a friend who had just been promoted to sergeant and assigned to an investigative unit after having spent their entire career in patrol. They were somewhat nervous about the prospects of supervising personnel who were performing duties that they themselves had never done. As we talked, the investigative manager told me that he hadn't seen one of his investigators for about a week and that every time he had spoken to this investigator he always seemed to be "working on the same case." I asked my friend if he had checked the case file to read the reports which reflected this nearly constant activity, and he said no. The next day he called back to say that he had looked at the case file, and the only document in it was the original field report from the patrol unit. After a few minutes I could almost hear the proverbial "light bulb" go on over his head when he stated "Hey, I think this guy is scamming me." Of course I agreed, and explained that investigators like this one were the reason that things like accountability mechanisms and case review had been invented. He learned his lesson, and fortunately for him it was learned rather early in the assignment before any permanent damage had occurred.

- **Inability to properly assign cases or prioritize assignments or cases**- with no investigative background, knowing which are the most important cases to assign can be very difficult. Of course, it stands to reason that the most serious cases need investigative work done before the less serious cases, but what does one do with two similar robberies or burglaries? In addition, assignment of cases, as discussed in Chapter 8, is a very important element of the case management process. Failure to assign cases appropriately can result in less-than-desirable outcomes of investigative efforts.

In addition to this, the "Out of Left Field" investigative manager probably doesn't have any really accurate assessment of the talents, abilities, or special skills of their personnel, which makes case assignment difficult. Sometimes this lack of knowledge can be addressed by inquiries of prior investigative managers or by a careful review of the various investigator's cases or backgrounds, but these are not foolproof.

- **Perhaps the biggest obstacle to success, however, is lack of credibility with subordinates**- the investigative personnel are well aware of the fact that their investigative manager hasn't "been there" and has never "done that," which can make for a very difficult situation for the new investigative manager. This lack of credibility can be manifested in several ways–the investigative personnel can simply "do their own thing" and not really listen to or take direction from the new manager, they can try to circumvent the new manager and go around him or her up the chain of command, or they can figure out a way to "submarine" the new manager with the hopes of ultimately getting rid of him or her. None of these are beneficial to the new investigative manager, but in most cases they are avoidable.

When personnel perceive their manager to have low credibility, they are much more likely to:

- **Produce only when being "watched"**- this is due to the lack of commitment to the goals of the unit or organization. This impacts investigative assignments negatively in many ways; cases do not receive the "personal attention" that they deserve, victims and witnesses are not given the proper level of empathetic treatment, and investigative documentation is sometimes completed in a less than thorough or even "lackadaisical" manner.

- **Be motivated primarily by extrinsic rewards,** such as money or overtime, than by the professional efforts of the unit. The unit that I mentioned earlier occurred in the mid-70s, prior to police unions, mandatory overtime, or many of the personnel improvements which have taken place over the past 35 years. Perhaps it was because we weren't receiving these things that we didn't consider them to be primary motivators, but the success of the unit was our primary motivator. Lest someone think that this statement shows that I'm "longing for the good old days", that's not true. Advancements in working conditions, salaries, and overtime compensation throughout my own career have dramatically improved the law enforcement profession. There is something to be said, however, for the personnel in a unit considering things other than compensation as important.
- **Say good things about the organization or unit publicly, but criticize it privately.** Cops complain–it's a fact of life, and I would be very concerned if they didn't. What they complain about, however, is the key. Personnel who perceive their manager to have little or no credibility often spend their time complaining about how the unit or organization is being managed, which can be very detrimental to the functioning of the unit. This is particularly true when dealing with an investigative unit, where unit cohesiveness and "esprit di corps" is critical.
- **Feel unsupported and unappreciated by the organization**-personnel who perceive their unit leader to have little or no credibility can sometimes have the feeling that the organization must not care at all about the unit or the personnel in it, based on the assignment of this "know-nothing" to the position of investigative manager. The importance of the unit is questioned, as are the unit's efforts, which can be very destructive.

For many newly assigned investigative managers who come from the "Out of Left Field" background, the problems that occur in their new assignment are not only initiated, but they are often compounded by them. In many cases, due to their lack of investigative background, insecurity, or nervousness, they fall back on what has worked for them in the past, and revert to the management style that worked well with patrol personnel. This can be disastrous, in that many of the supervisory and management strategies that work very well with patrol don't work at all with investigative personnel, and investigative managers who try to apply them usually fail miserably.

During my years as a young cop, I spent the majority of my time in investigative assignments. I was promoted several times from investigative assignments to management positions in investigative units. While this afforded me many of the advantages that were just mentioned, later in my career I was assigned to management of both patrol and investigative units in which I had no background. This could have been very difficult, as these personnel were performing duties and conducting investigations with which I had no familiarity whatsoever. In addition, I have been selected as a chief of police twice for departments in which I was an "outsider". These experiences have given me a pretty good idea of what the "Out of Left Field' investigative manager must be experiencing.

I have always believed that most cops are pretty fair-minded people, and if (you) the new manager can convince them that you're not there to hurt anyone, that they will all be treated fairly, and that they will be supported, most of them will give you a chance. The "Out of Left Field" investigative manager who comes to the investigative unit and professes to know things that they can't possibly know is making a huge mistake. Cops are the hardest people in the world to "con," and the investigative manager that tries to convince them that they have a background in doing something that they haven't really done will fail.

Rather than take this approach, I've always believed that a "little humility goes a long way," and to come into a new assignment and ask for help to get acclimated is not a sign of weakness, rather I see it as a sign of strength and good judgment. The best bosses I've ever had in my law enforcement career and in fact in my life all had one thing in common: they were all smart enough to know that they didn't know everything. Beyond that, however, and more importantly, they were also smart enough to know that they didn't have to know everything.

I've been giving the same basic opening speech to personnel in every unit I've ever managed, and they get it both verbally and in writing, as soon as I get to the new assignment. I give them a little background about myself, and make it very clear that I don't consider myself to be an "expert" in anything. I ask them to please help me to learn what I need to know to be successful in this new position, and to not ever be afraid to approach me or to make suggestions. I then ask them that if they see me walking into an electric fan to fight the urge to sit back and watch me get chopped up, but rather grab my shirt tail and pull me out of the fan. I've been in numerous situations in which I was told at the onset of the assignment that I'd be getting nothing but grief from personnel, and fortunately for me, that hasn't happened.

As a chief of police, I had an investigative manager (sergeant) who was getting reassigned to a new position, and needed someone to replace him. I took a look at an extremely professional and competent patrol sergeant and sat down with him to discuss the position. This sergeant had an outstanding background, and had done well in everything to which he was assigned. He also had an outstanding military background, having been assigned to some very critical positions while in the military. I had seen his military records when he was being considered for promotion to sergeant, and was very impressed. He immediately got very nervous, telling me that he had no investigative background, didn't want the transfer, and was quite happy where he was at in patrol. I replied that I am a firm believer in "succession planning," and that in order to maximize his chances for career advancement, and to maximize his value to the agency, that he at least seriously consider taking the assignment.

It took a while, but he ultimately indicated that he'd be willing to take the assignment as sergeant in the investigative unit. His biggest concern, which he confided in me, was being accepted by the investigators, who all knew that he had no investigative background whatsoever. He was particularly concerned about the senior investigator in the unit, who had a (well-deserved) reputation of being difficult to work with due to his being very surly, which occurred on a regular basis. This is not to say that he wasn't competent, which he was, but because of his moodiness and unpredictability, his coworkers often had to "walk on eggshells" around him.

I explained to the sergeant that there was no way he was going to convince the investigators assigned to the unit that he had any background in investigations because he didn't. He also could not convince them that he had any real in-depth knowledge of their jobs. I offered a suggestion, based on the "a little humility goes a long way" theory. I suggested that he call a meeting of all of the investigative personnel, which included general assignment investigators, school resource officers, and investigative personnel assigned to the various task forces. At the meeting he should outline his plans for supporting their efforts and he should make very clear what they already knew—he had no background whatsoever as an investigator. I suggested he then ask these personnel to teach what he needed to know to effectively manage the unit. Within a month, he was in my office briefing me on a serious ongoing investigation, when I asked him how the assignment was going. He smiled and said: "You know Chief, when you assigned me there I was convinced that you were a jerk and that I was probably never going to speak to you again, but this has been the most fun I've had in years." He performed extremely well in the assignment, and the fact that his background in the agency was expanded had an positive impact on his later career. Although it has been a number of years since this occurred, every time we get together he brings it up, and always mentions how surprised he was that it worked out to his benefit. I usually reply that "even a blind pig finds an acorn now and then," and even a guy like me sometimes makes a good call.

The manner in which one supervises investigative personnel utilizes the same principles as the supervision of any other police personnel. While the principles are the same, the strategies and techniques will differ quite a bit. These differences are dictated by the position itself, and investigative managers who don't recognize these differences are doomed to failure. The supervision of investigative personnel will be discussed in Chapter 7.

Chapter 2

CRIMINAL INVESTIGATIONS: THE BASICS

To manage an investigative unit, you must first have a clear under-standing of what encompasses a criminal investigation, including both primary and secondary goals. This is particularly critical for the investigative manager who is not an experienced investigator. When you understand the basics, you can begin the process of managing.

WHAT IS A CRIMINAL INVESTIGATION?

The term *criminal investigation* means different things to different people. For the purposes of this chapter and this book, a criminal investigation consists of police activity directed at two things:

1. Apprehension of criminals by gathering evidence leading to their arrest
2. Collection and presentation of evidence and testimony resulting in conviction of the perpetrator.

The basic goals of the investigative unit in any criminal investigation are fairly straightforward. They are to identify, apprehend, and convict the perpetrator. There are secondary goals as well that the manager of the investigative unit should never overlook:

- **Clearing additional crimes**—Many offenders such as burglars, bad check passers, and auto thieves are usually very prolific. They generally don't stop committing their criminal specialties until they are forced to. This is probably because these types of criminals are often very successful until they are caught. When one becomes very adept at committing a certain type of crime that's profitable, why stop?

- **Recovering stolen property**–I've often heard both patrol officers and investigators state that they sometimes feel they work for insurance companies, simply taking reports for stolen property so that a claim can be filed by the victim. Often stolen property is never found. However, on some occasions, proceeds are recovered and the victim gets the benefit of having his or her property returned.

- **Preventing additional crimes**–This takes place in a variety of ways. When a very prolific and active criminal is arrested, many additional crimes are probably prevented. Even if an offender is not arrested, the mere fact that they have been identified might cause them to refrain from committing additional crimes.

- **Gathering intelligence information**–Unfortunately, this is probably one of the most overlooked, albeit one of the most important, secondary goals. Gathering intelligence information is something that should not only be written into the job description, it should be practiced every day by every member of the department. Each and every time an investigator works an investigation he or she should consider the intelligence information that could be gathered that could help with other or future investigations.

   Intelligence information is something that is often misunderstood. The best definition I've heard came from an instructor in one of the first military intelligence courses I ever took. He said that "the art of intelligence is gathering seemingly unrelated bits and pieces of information which are then collected, collated, studied, and analyzed in an effort to provide direction for future decision making." Intelligence information is like gold: It's great to have and the more you have the more you should want. Investigators who fail to consider this one of their secondary goals are missing out on an opportunity to make their jobs more effective, easier, and much more enjoyable. Collecting and properly utilizing intelligence information allows investigators to approach their investigations with the greatest chance of success. Gathering intelligence may be as simple as researching all reports, field interview cards, traffic stops, or any other document where a suspect might be named or included. Although most of the information might not amount to anything or provide any worthwhile direction, there is the chance that one little bit of the information might lead to solving the case.

- **Training patrol personnel**–This is also one of the most overlooked, albeit one of the most important, secondary goals. Some of the more common complaints include report writing, witness handling, crime scene and/or evidence management, and poorly conducted preliminary investigations. These things all have something in common if you stop to think about them. If these things aren't done correctly, the job of the follow-up investigator becomes much more difficult.

    Rather than continuing to complain about the deficiencies, what about doing something about it? How about assigning an investigator to take samples of well-written witness statements to roll calls and discuss them with patrol officers and their supervisors? In addition, how are patrol officers supposed to learn the latest M.O.s of criminals if nobody teaches them? Why not present photos of the latest methods of secreting drugs in vehicles, or the newest methods in retagging stolen autos, or the latest twists in identity theft, or a variety of other items that patrol officers encounter on a daily basis? Not only is this a golden opportunity to teach them something useful, it can go a long way in improving investigator/patrol officer relationships.

THE INVESTIGATIVE PROCESS

A criminal investigation is a process. The importance of viewing it as such, rather than as a single event, cannot be overstated. Some investigative managers see their responsibility as merely assigning cases and forgetting them until they're concluded. Nothing could be farther from the truth. Every element in the process is critical not only to the success of the individual investigation but also to the overall success of the investigative unit.

The process begins when the police become aware of the offense and ends with the presentation of the completed investigation to prosecutors or some other administrative closing. The means by which the police become aware of the offense will either be proactively or reactively. *Proactively* would include self-initiated investigations, or investigations that originate as offshoots of ongoing investigations. The most obvious examples include self-initiated drug and vice investigations, and gang crimes investigations that are initiated through information gained during other investigations. *Reactively* would include cases in which the police respond to an offense that has already occurred. These constitute the bulk of the investigative effort for most agencies.

Two key parts of the investigative process are the *preliminary investigation* and the follow-up investigation. Typically, the preliminary investigation consists of the following elements:

1. Providing aid to the injured
2. Protecting the scene to ensure that evidence is not lost or contaminated
3. Determining if an offense has actually been committed and, if so, the exact nature of the offense
4. Determining the identity of the suspect or suspects and making an arrest if it can be accomplished at the scene or through immediate pursuit
5. Furnishing other units with descriptions, method and direction of flight, and other relevant information regarding wanted persons or vehicles. This is accomplished through the communications center.
6. Obtaining complete identification of all witnesses
7. Determining the need for investigative specialists and assistance
8. Compiling a thorough and accurate report of activities.

The *follow-up investigation* usually consists of the following elements:

1. Identifying and apprehending the offender
2. Arranging for the analysis and evaluation of evidence
3. Recovering stolen property
4. In-depth interviewing of victims and witnesses
5. Interrogating suspects
6. Determining the involvement of the suspect in additional crimes
7. Recording information obtained
8. Preparing the case for court presentation.

Criminal investigations are a challenge because crime does not occur on a schedule. If we knew, for example, that all burglaries took place between 3 AM and 4 AM in the morning in light industrial areas, we could easily assign patrol officers to stake out these areas and catch the burglars. This would make it very simple. We wouldn't have to trouble investigators to do follow-up investigations as there wouldn't be any need for follow-up investigations. Because of the chance occurrence of crime, no single element or unit of the police department can be charged with every investigation. Selecting the unit to which each investigative duty is assigned should be based on three considerations:

1. **Economy of manpower**–Manpower is expensive and should be utilized to the department's best advantage. When I teach classes and discuss this topic, I conduct an informal survey among investigator supervisors and commanders and ask how many of them have enough investigators to address the needs of their agencies. Over the course of many years of teaching and probably thousands of students, I have yet to see a hand raised in answer to the question.

   In other words, seldom if ever are there enough investigators to handle everything that comes along. It's imperative that the available manpower is utilized in the most responsible, efficient, and effective manner possible. We've only got so many investigators to work assigned cases. If we assign them to matters that really don't warrant their unique expertise and abilities, we're wasting their expertise.

2. **Immediate availability of service**–When conducting follow-up investigations, time can be of the essence. There often seems to be a correlation between the likelihood of arrest and prosecution and the time it takes for the investigation to begin. As a very young investigator working on one of my first homicides, an experienced Chicago Police Department violent crimes investigator once told me about the 48-hour rule. His experience was that if you didn't get a handle on whodunnit within the first 48 hours after discovery of the murder, your chances for finding the perpetrator diminished rapidly. Not knowing if this theory was the result of any empirical research, I took it at face value. Over the years, I've seen the logic behind this rule demonstrated several

times. The chances of success in a follow-up does seem to depend heavily on how quickly the police begin their investigation.

3. **Effectiveness of performance**–Assignments should be made to the units within the police department best qualified to perform the task. In other words, you wouldn't assign a juvenile case to an evidence technician if a juvenile officer was available. Nor would you assign a child sex crimes case to an accident reconstruction-ist if a child sex crimes investigator was available. The responsi-bility for the various elements of the investigative process must be specifically assigned to specific elements or units within the police department. I strongly recommend that this be done *in writing* as part of police department policy. (See the example provided in Appendix 1.) If this is not done, neglect through oversight and/or friction due to duplication of efforts will occur. Sergeants from patrol will battle with investigators over who is responsible for preliminary investigations, how far these preliminaries should go, exactly what entails the preliminary, and a variety of other issues.

RAND STUDY ON INVESTIGATIONS

A number of years ago, the Rand Corporation did a study centered around the value of the traditional investigative unit in terms of crime solving and contributions to the overall role of the police agency. Although over 25 years old, the findings and recommendations of the study are as relevant today as they were then. The study looked at police departments, from small to very large, in several locations with-in the United States resulted in many findings. First, *clearance rates by investigative divisions are unreliable.* Most crimes were cleared during the initial investigation by patrol officers, yet many agencies relegate the role of the patrol officer to that of a "crime reporter."

Second, *many reported felonies receive no more than superficial attention.* In many places, minor property crimes are seldom if ever investigat-ed, even if the value of the stolen property is at whatever dollar amount of property value constitutes felony level. Yet many agencies waste investigators' time by having them go over these cases. Once I was teaching a class where almost all of the students were from the same agency, a very large one that had nearly 1,500 personnel. We were discussing caseloads for investigators, and several of the burglary sergeants told me that their investigators typically carried 200–300 cases each. I was astounded, and even more so when they told me that each and every burglary to a structure (house, apartment building, garage, business) in their city was the subject of a follow-up investigation and was assigned to an investigator. They went on to explain that rarely did any of these cases actually get solved, and that their investigators spent most of their days shuffling the stack of cases from one side of their desks to the other. The bottom-line explanation was that their mayor had promised in a campaign that all property crimes would be investigated by an investigator, and all they were doing was following the mayor's directions. Perhaps this was not the most efficient use of investigative resources.

A third finding was that, *for many cases, there is a serious gap between the prosecutor and the investigator.* Key evidence that could help the prosecutor is not always properly documented by the investigator. There are many agencies, unfortunately, that have little or no contact with the prosecutors other than to hand the cases over to them.

Finally, *too much time is spent locating witnesses and reviewing reports on cases that have no logical chance of ever being solved.* The conclusion you can draw from this is that a number of cases that should not be assigned to investigators are being assigned anyway. Clearly this is a waste of time and a poor use of the most important resource you have: manpower.

Realistically, if the mayor's garage gets burglarized and the only thing taken is a 15-year-old lawnmower with no identifying characteristics or serial numbers, you will probably have to assign investigators to the investigation. There are many unsolvable cases that must be investigated anyway due to the nature of the offense, the status of the victim, location the crime occurred, and so on. Fortunately, those cases seem to be few and far between.

As with most studies, when there are findings, there are also recommendations. Some of the recommendations are as follows:

1. **Screen cases.** Without the use of some type of case screening, *all investigations* are assigned for follow-up and a great deal of time is wasted by investigators investigating cases that have no real chance of ever being solved. Case screening identifies those cases where the solvability potential is favorable. There are currently

several instruments and reports available, most of which are based on some type of a point system, for determining when enough evidence or potential investigative leads exist to warrant follow-up investigations. Points are given for things such as identifiable stolen property, available witnesses, possible offender/vehicle descriptions, and so on. If a certain threshold number of points exist, the case is assigned for follow-up. We will discuss how this case screening might take place in Chapter 8.

Regardless of what type of case screening is used, make follow-up contact with victims. Crime victims aren't concerned that the police department and the investigative unit are using their limited resources in the most responsible manner; all they care about is receiving professional and somewhat personalized service. Without this follow-up contact, victims sometimes feel like they've been lost in the shuffle and are being treated like a number instead of a person whose privacy and property have been somehow violated.

2. **Manage the criminal investigation process.** As stated earlier, the criminal investigation is not a single event but a process with many interdependent elements. All of these elements, including initial report review, case screening, case assignment, case review, and case referral, require your careful management. Lack of administrative control over the continuing investigative process undoubtedly leads to many shortcomings, such as inequitable caseloads, improper assignment of cases, incorrect priority decisions, and lack of investigative continuity.

3. **Improve police/prosecutor relations.** Don't take the attitude that "now we've referred the case to the prosecutors, it's not our problem anymore." Successful investigation and prosecution of criminal offenses is a team effort. Without a doubt, the relationship between police and prosecutors is symbiotic. The two entities, although apparently separate, are interdependent and mutually beneficial to each other. This concept is so critical that it should be reinforced as often as possible with all investigators. The police, no matter how talented they might be, are not capable of prosecuting cases by themselves. Prosecutors, no matter how talented they might be, are not capable of investigating cases, arresting offenders, conducting interviews, and all the other things that go into a criminal investigation.

4. **Enhance the investigative role of the patrol officer.** We should definitely get away from the idea that patrol officers are merely "reporters of crime" and that they should be excluded from the investigative process. Trained police officers are capable enough to conduct preliminary investigations on all offenses and complete investigations on some offenses. We are doing them a disservice if we treat them as anything less. And, as the next chapter discusses, we end up doing ourselves a disservice as well.

Chapter 3

THE ROLE OF PATROL IN THE INVESTIGATIVE PROCESS

Investigative managers quickly realize that the initial stages of the investigative process are critical to the potential success of follow-up investigative efforts. If these initial steps are not taken correctly, the difficulty associated with the follow-up investigation often becomes overwhelming. This is why professionalism on the part of the patrol unit in the initial stages of the investigative process is absolutely essential. Although some agencies feel the patrol unit should not be involved in the investigative process, in reality patrol is the logical unit to conduct preliminary investigations of all crimes and, for certain crimes, complete investigations.

PATROL OFFICERS AND PRELIMINARY INVESTIGATIONS

As a young officer, one of the first things I was taught about preliminary investigative work by patrol officers at crime scenes was to remember three simple rules:

1. Put your hands in your pockets.
2. Don't chew gum or smoke.
3. For heaven's sake, don't touch anything.

There are probably some agencies that are still teaching their personnel this "mantra," with the same results: patrol officers that don't do *anything* to initiate preliminary investigative efforts. This is sad. When you consider that the average police department probably spends over $20,000 to recruit, test, process, examine, train, and equip new patrol officers, not utilizing them except as expensive security guards at crime scenes doesn't seem to be the most fiscally responsible thing to do. Every officer who has concluded his or her field training program should be capable of conducting a thorough and professional preliminary investigation. Even so, some agencies feel that the patrol unit has no business becoming involved in the investigative process. In reality, though, patrol is the logical unit to be assigned responsibility for conducting preliminary investigations of all crimes and, for certain crimes, complete investigations. Why is this true?

First of all, *patrol is on duty 24 hours a day*, while most agencies don't have the luxury of having investigators on duty at all times. Many smaller agencies are relegated to having investigators on duty only during the day shift. Some mid-sized and most large agencies have them on duty on days and afternoons, and for the largest agencies, during the midnight shift. Patrol, on the other hand, is already there. And if their officers are well trained, they should be able to start the investigative process so that the follow-up investigation is based on some good preliminary work.

This leads to a second reason. *Patrol personnel can conduct or at least begin investigations at once.* Utilizing patrol can avoid holding investigations until a investigator comes on duty. Chapter 1 discussed how there seems to be a correlation between how quickly an investigation starts and the chance of success. If delays initiating the investigation are minimized, our chances for successful follow-up investigations are maximized. So, what are the advantages of using patrol in the investigative process? There are five primary ones:

1. **Relieves the investigative unit of a great deal of preliminary digging and many routine cases.** Properly trained patrol officers are capable of securing the crime scene (if one exists), handling and interviewing victims and witnesses, and initiating the investigative process. There are a number of situations in which patrol can actually *solve* the crime themselves, with no assistance from the investigative unit. This leads to the second advantage.

2. **Leads to the more efficient and constructive use of time by investigative units.** When patrol officers conduct good preliminary investigations, the associated follow-up investigations are

sometimes very limited or maybe even unnecessary. Investigators can then spend their time on only those matters that actually require investigative expertise, and not on every crime that occurs.

3. **Broadens the experience and training of patrol officers.** It allows them to expand their horizons by getting involved in more than just patrol. This can be of great benefit to not only them but to the entire agency.

4. **Allows patrol personnel to demonstrate their individual abilities.** This can be very useful for their consideration for future assignments. Considering the fact that our investigators come from our patrol officers, how else will we have any idea of their potential for investigative assignments if we don't allow them to demonstrate these abilities as patrol officers?

5. **Improves morale.** This may be the most important advantage. The patrol officer feels more like a part of the department. This can increase not only the morale of the individual officer involved in the investigation, but also the morale of the rest of the patrol force.

For example, many police departments now require patrol officer applicants to complete college credits prior to applying for a position. Having a college degree does not make one a better person or even potentially a better cop. However, we must take into consideration that hiring well-educated people most likely means these people will become bored easily if their duties consist exclusively of routine and occasionally mundane assignments. This problem is exacerbated when something exciting happens, like a real crime, and they are relegated to standing around and not doing much of anything. This is hardly the proper method for retaining these young people in our profession.

When you consider that these highly educated people are suddenly told that when something important occurs that they are to stand by and do *pretty much* nothing, is there any wonder why they sometimes leave police agencies?

MODELS FOR USING PATROL

Although the role of the patrol officer in criminal investigation varies greatly from agency to agency, there seem to be certain models of these roles that include things like the responsibility of patrol, case referral procedures, and management policies. Naturally, there are pros and cons to each of these different models.

Basic Model

Unfortunately, there are still many departments who utilize what I call the basic model. In this model, the responsibility of patrol is to prepare and complete a basic report. All cases are referred, including preliminary investigations. This model is probably the easiest from the standpoint of management policies, as the policy directive can be very short: Patrol will do nothing at the scene of a crime except wait for investigators to arrive. The referral procedure is also simple, because everything is referred. The consequences of this model, however, are all negative. It is likely that insufficient data will be collected. It's hard enough to get witnesses to remain at a crime scene and talk to the police, but if these witnesses are forced to stand around waiting for an investigator to arrive, the witnesses probably won't be in any mood to cooperate if they do bother to stick around. This model also lends itself to create low morale among patrol officers.

I remember an incident involving a young state trooper who was particularly aggressive and initiated a great deal of enforcement activity beyond traffic enforcement. He was traveling on a Chicago expressway and passed an (apparently) disabled vehicle on the opposite shoulder. He intended to exit at the next ramp, re-enter the expressway going in the opposite direction, and process the car for later towing. As he exited, he noted from the overpass that a car containing two individuals had pulled over behind the disabled vehicle. Both subjects exited and began removing parts including the wheels and battery from the disabled vehicle, which they deposited in the trunk of their vehicle. The trooper, although driving a clearly marked squad car, set up a surveillance of the activity from the overpass, approximately an eighth of a mile away. He called for backup and captured the unsuspecting vehicle burglars. Not only did he recover the parts from the disabled vehicle, but he also recovered a weapon and some drugs and syringes from the burglars' vehicle.

I happened to be at the station when he brought in his prisoners for processing. I offered to help him process the prisoners and the evidence. While we were doing so, his immediate supervisor entered the processing room. The trooper spread the drugs and the weapon out on the desk, exclaiming, "Look what I got, Sarge . . . drugs, guns, and two mutts on a vehicle burglary!" The sergeant uttered what I consider to be one of the greatest examples of poor management I have heard before or since. The sergeant said, "Look kid, you're out there to write tickets and stop overweight trucks. Leave this other crap for the investigators." I watched the face of that young trooper, justifiably full of pride, quickly turn to exasperation and then disgust. He started to deflate like a balloon with a small pinhole in it. I remember filing that verbal interchange in the back of my mind as one of the things not to do if and when I ever made sergeant. The number of self-initiated activities that young trooper became involved in diminished rapidly, and he ultimately left law enforcement and opened a service station about a year later. What a preventable loss!

I happened to see that former trooper a number of years later, and he confided in me that it was that specific incident that convinced him to leave law enforcement, and that he still misses the law enforcement profession. He felt that this was an omen of things to come, not only with this supervisor, but with the agency that the supervisor represented. Ultimately, he became very successful and somewhat wealthy, but that one stupid comment by that sergeant took what could have been an outstanding law enforcement career and destroyed it.

When morale plummets, it stands to reason that the level of productivity among patrol officers soon goes with it. If, after having jumped through all the hoops to become a cop, the new patrol officer realizes that he or she isn't viewed as intelligent enough to do *anything* but wait for an investigator when a real crime occurs, how much effort do you think they're going to expend in their daily duties?

Expanded-Use-of-Patrol Model

A better model is one where the role of the patrol officer is somewhat enhanced and they are given the opportunity to put all of that education, academy training, and field training experience to good use. There are several strategies to enhance the role of the patrol officer. I will highlight some aspects of several of them.

In all of these strategies, patrol is responsible for conducting a thorough preliminary investigation and completing a detailed report. The patrol officer and his or her supervisor decide whether to call forensics or evidence specialists. The officer and supervisor also recommend either closing the case or referring it for follow-up investigations by investigators. Patrol is charged with investigating crimes in selected categories beyond their initial investigative phase. Sometimes, closure can occur on scene after initial investigation by patrol.

The case referral procedure in these models is a little more complicated than in the basic model. The investigative manager takes into account the recommendation of the patrol supervisor and, using some type of case screening criteria, decides on assignment for follow-up investigation or closure. Only cases that would involve extensive follow-up, require a high level of skill, or are of an exceptional nature are referred. Management in this model includes establishing policies and procedures for case screening, the investigative role of patrol, and the follow-up role of investigators. You must also define categories where patrol is responsible for full investigations. Adapting a case screening system that incorporates early, on-scene, case-closure criteria is essential for this strategy to work.

This model also requires additional training for both patrol and investigative unit supervisors so that the process flows smoothly. This is particularly true in departments transitioning from the basic model to a system in which the role of patrol is enhanced. Unlike the basic model, all the consequences of this model are positive in nature. Resources of the investigative unit will be better utilized as those (usually limited) resources can focus only on "solvable" cases. Another positive consequence is that this model creates an interdependency between the patrol and investigative divisions. They actually need each other: Investigators need patrol to conduct thorough preliminaries and detailed reports so that they might conduct their follow-ups, and patrol needs investigators to continue what they've started to its logical conclusion. Investigators, now that they are no longer swamped with preliminary tasks on investigations, can actually focus their time on matters that need their expertise. This model permits investigators to increase their specialties or to adopt new roles. Perhaps most importantly, this model enhances patrol's morale and productivity. No longer are the patrol officers relegated to the position of "reporters of crime"; they are actually involved in *solving* crimes.

Even during follow-up investigations, the patrol unit should be used as much as possible for such tasks as checking locations, canvassing neighborhoods, looking for vehicles or suspects, and other noninvestigative duties. By involving the patrol officers in the process, the effectiveness of the (usually limited manpower) investigative unit is multiplied. Get involved in the patrol roll calls, provide them with the information you're seeking, and you'll be amazed at what the patrol officers will uncover for you.

A team of investigators from a suburban police department was searching for a suspect of a particularly violent home invasion in which the victim was an elderly retired court clerk, very well known in the law enforcement community. The investigators, with other cases to work, were having limited success. The information on the suspect was turned over to the patrol unit and within three days the midnight shift had the suspect in custody. It wasn't that the investigators looking for the suspect weren't competent; they were simply too busy to devote all of their time to the search. The patrol officers used their spare time, particularly during nontraditional hours, to "shake the bushes" and locate the suspect. The positive morale benefits to the entire department generated by this capture were truly amazing.

Finally, consider the following scenario. Patrol Officer A works a midnight shift, gets his or her couple of movers to keep the sergeant happy, and then is dispatched to a burglar alarm at a local business. Patrol Officer A is assigned to stand by the door and wait for investigators. When the investigators arrive, he or she leaves to go back on patrol.

Patrol Officer B is working the same midnight shift in a more progressive agency. He, too, handles his beat and then is dispatched to a burglar alarm at a local business. Patrol Officer B knows he is part of the investigative process, so he knows more is expected of him. Patrol Officer B takes more care securing the scene, arranges for someone to go around a two-block radius of the business and obtain license plates from parked cars in the area, helps interview potential witnesses, awaits the arrival of the business owner, and also waits for the investigators. When the investigators arrive, he has a great deal of preliminary information for them, which will be reduced to a detailed report of his preliminary investigation. If this patrol officer is really sharp, he also arranges for copies of all field interview cards and traffic citations that occurred in the area around the time that the burglary was believed to have occurred to be forwarded to investigators for use in the follow-up investigation. The point of the illustration is which patrol officer do you think has better morale? Which officer do you think has more chance of overcoming the occasionally mind-numbing routine of patrol and finishing out his or her career with a positive attitude? Which officer do you think feels more like a true part of the department? I'll go with Officer B.

Chapter 4

ORGANIZING THE INVESTIGATIVE UNIT

The organization of the investigative unit has an important bearing on the unit's efficiency and the ultimate success of the investigators. As such, how you organize the unit should not be taken lightly. To maximize the unit's effectiveness and efficiency, carefully consider how the investigative unit fits into the overall goals and objectives of the agency.

SPECIALIZED VERSUS NONSPECIALIZED

Unfortunately, the mobility and sophistication of modern criminals seems to be growing at an alarming rate. In response, some police agencies tend to overspecialize their criminal investigative units. Even some small police departments have seen fit to specialize their investigative units to the point of being somewhat ludicrous, considering the types of crimes that occur in their jurisdictions and the number of investigators that they have to do the work. Where this specialization might increase the effectiveness in a given area (limited though it might be), it can often result in less manpower for general investigations. A similar phenomenon has occurred in the medical field. As a child, I can remember doctors making house calls. Most doctors were general practitioners who could treat a variety of maladies for the entire family. It seems that for a number of years, this type of physician became a dying breed while the various specialties blossomed. Over the past few years, however, I have noticed that there seems to be a "new" specialty emerging called family practice. Maybe we're going back to a time when the same physician can treat a variety of maladies for the entire family.

When determining how to organize the investigative unit and taking specialization of investigators into account, a good rule of thumb is to have as few specialized units as possible, staffed with as few people as practical. Specialization of investigative units is usually done by either function or geography. For smaller agencies, the question of geography is often a moot point. Smaller agencies usually do not have geographic divisions for the various parts of the community. All personnel work out of the same facility because the distances encountered in the community are not excessive.

The same goes for specialization by function. With many smaller agencies, the general assignment nature of the investigative unit dictates that all investigators must be capable of investigating a wide variety of offenses. The lack of manpower precludes you from breaking down the types of crimes to be investigated into specialized units. In larger agencies with more investigators, the specialization by function might be workable. Basic specialization by function involves:

- Crimes against property (burglary, theft, auto theft)
- Crimes against persons (murder, rape, robbery, other sex crimes)
- General assignment (bad checks, con games, forgery).

Whether specialization is by function or geography, use caution to ensure that specialization doesn't develop to the point where work is unfairly assigned. Investigators who are assigned to work a specialty will notice immediately if their caseload is substantially higher than other investigators in other specialty assignments.

Regardless of specialization, however, I believe that investigators should be generally capable of investigating all categories of crimes and assist each other when necessary. When a major crime occurs and investigators from the entire unit are assigned, it is very beneficial to know that the investigator assigned to handling bad checks can also assist in a homicide investigation if needed. There are pros and cons to specialization in investigative units. The pros include:

- **Criminals are specialized.** Criminals tend to perfect their own offenses. Particularly if they are successful, they rarely change their own specialties. Successful burglars, for example, don't often decide one morning to become auto thieves, and successful forgers don't often venture into the world of armed robbery.

- **Investigators working on a few types of crimes become experts.** They become experts in looking for clues or in understanding M.O.s regarding their specialty. Specialists also often become expert in the law regarding their specialty, to the point where they may be more familiar with the laws on specific crimes than the prosecutors.
- **Specialists become very familiar with the criminals operating in that specialty.** They become so effective that they can sometimes deduce an offender's involvement by either the M.O. or the area worked. Investigators who specialize in a limited number of types of crimes often generate their own personal database of criminals and can pretty much pinpoint the types of offenses in which these criminals are involved.

While working on a rape investigation as a young investigator, I was referred to a suburban investigator widely regarded as an expert in investigating these types of crimes. After I related the specifics of the case to him, he asked me for very specific information regarding the offense, such as the exact words used by the offender and the exact sequence of the sexual assault committed by this depraved individual. After I finished, he thought for a minute and gave me the name of a possible offender, stating, "If this clown's not still in the joint, he's probably your guy." I remember walking out of the police station thinking to myself, "This investigator is either some type of psychic or he's completely full of it." Well, the former was true. He had deduced the identity of the offender based on the M.O., and within a week we had our offender in custody.

There are also some cons that go along with specialization in investigative units. These include:

- **Specialization can lead to an elitist attitude.** Specialists may view themselves as smarter or better than generalists. This can have a devastating impact on the overall morale of the unit.

  In one assignment, I managed an investigative unit consisting of two general assignment squads and two specialty squads of investigators. It quickly became apparent that one of the general assignment squads had some extremely talented investigators who were successful in the investigation of violent crimes. Their success rate in handling homicides, violent sexual assaults, and similar offenses was remarkable. They were all very street-smart, had many effective confidential informants, were excellent interviewers, and had excellent instincts that helped greatly in solving these types of cases. Soon I began assigning an increasing number of the more violent crimes to this particular squad. This seemed to work well until we were inundated with a large number of background investigations to conduct on police officer applicants. It was customary to assign these backgrounds evenly, but when I assigned a group of these backgrounds to the squad working the violent crimes, I was met with a great deal of resistance because they were "violent crimes investigators who didn't have time for these B.S. background investigations." Needless to say, they were quickly shown the error of their thinking and instructed to complete the backgrounds. It then struck me that I had created these "prima donnas" and it was my fault that they felt they were too important for the more "mundane" assignments. It was a very important management lesson for me.

- **Specialization can lead to situations where specialists can't function outside of their specialty.** Some specialists seem to be so immersed in their specialty that they lose the ability to function in other areas of investigations. This dramatically diminishes their overall worth to the investigative unit and can cause serious issues if they are transferred, promoted, or returned to a patrol assignment. Although it is your responsibility to give the assignment to the most qualified person, it is also true that any police investigator should be capable of handling a general assignment investigation.

  This problem seems to be particularly true in narcotics enforcement. Although a truly good narcotics investigator is exposed to a variety of tasks involved in any type of investigation, such as report writing, surveillance, interviewing, evidence handling, and so on, it also seems true that being totally immersed in the persona of working narcotics can make them less effective when investigating other types of crimes.

I worked with an extremely talented investigator who was assigned as the squad supervisor for a group of narcotics agents. He had gotten into a very violent shoot-out very early in his career and was "reward-ed" by being assigned to the narcotics task force. After twenty years at the task force, he was nearing retirement and his department advised him that he would be coming back to regular patrol or investigative duties for his last year on the job. He was devastated, came running into my office and asked me to somehow mediate his situation as he didn't think he could work "straight" investigations any more, and he was absolutely certain that he could never go back to being a patrol officer. As talented as he was, the fact that he was in a specialized assignment for an extremely long time had convinced him that nar-cotics was the only function that he could perform. It really didn't mat-ter that in actuality he was talented enough to perform any assign-ment, in his mind he wasn't, and as often occurs, perception became reality.

- **Specialization can lead to inequitable caseloads.** If the inves-tigative unit is overspecialized to the point that it doesn't accu-rately reflect the types of crimes encountered and referred for investigation, you may be faced with specialists who are sitting around until a case involving their particular specialty comes along while the general assignment investigators are swamped with cases.

 Many police departments, including some smaller agencies, get caught up in what I call the new initiative syndrome. In this sce-nario, whenever a new crime wave comes along, the agency feels compelled to create some type of specialist or specialty unit to address these crimes. This might not be a bad idea, but if none of these crimes actually occur in the community, the training dollars are wasted on people who are extremely talented, with nothing to investigate.

- **Specialization can sometimes stifle the career of the special-ist.** This is particularly true if the specialist is successful. In other words, this specialist is being punished for being effective and doing his or her job well. Sometimes the people who are the most successful in a specialty aren't even considered for promotion or other career-enhancing assignments because of their success in their particular specialty. They get passed over and are still expect-ed to continue to perform at a high level.

 Unfortunately, this often has a disproportionately negative impact on female and minority investigators. It is also more frequent in assignments such as undercover or narcotics. Female and minority investigators who are successful in these assignments sometimes remain in them even when a transfer to a more mainstream assignment might be better for their career. This not only negatively impacts the particular investigator but the overall organization as well, particularly when these successful investigators begin to feel that they are being used because of their gender or ethnic background. This perception of unfair treatment, whether accurate or not, can cause even the most dedicated and hardworking investigators to slack off their otherwise high quality of work.

I worked with an extremely professional Federal Agent who was almost "legendary" in his particular agency for his expertise in undercover operations. I knew this agent extremely well, as he and I had attended high school together and we had worked a number of undercover operations together, and I found his skill at the undercover role was truly amazing. As our careers went on, I moved on to supervisory and administrative positions, and he stayed with the undercover work. At first this was by his own choice, but later he began to notice that he was "conveniently" not notified of supervisory openings, nor was he ever encouraged to apply for promotions into supervisory positions. In reality, he had become "too good to give up," and it was becoming very stifling to his career. At the time of his retirement, he told me that he felt that his agency had in effect "punished him for doing a good job" at the undercover assignments by not encouraging or supporting him in moving up the chain of command.

I have always felt that if someone in a specialty position truly *wants to stay there* knowing full well that it could prove stifling to their career and might limit their opportunities for promotion or different assignments, then so be it. The problem comes when it is the agency management that makes that decision for the specialist, rather than allowing them to consciously make it for themselves. This can lead to frustration and a very negative feeling toward their agency. Punishing people who perform well is not hardly an enlightened management philosophy, and it can be extremely destructive, not only to those personnel who are directly impacted, but to the rest of the personnel. When people see that the top performers in an organization are treated poorly, the incentive for them to become top performers diminishes.

A number of years ago I attended a management class and the instructor began discussing how employees often fit into various categories. The example he used was the "10–80–10 Principle," where three groups exist: 10% top performers, 10% poor performers, and 80% were what he called "maintainers." These "maintainers" were neither extremely good or extremely bad, they just came to work and did their jobs. The more I thought about it, I came to the conclusion that he was correct, but I thought that there was a better way to describe these categories.

The top 10% are what I would consider effective. They get to work early, stay late, never complain, and give at least 100% of their efforts all the time, no matter what.

The bottom 10% are what I would consider defective. They get to work late, do very little while they are there, regularly cause trouble in the workplace, and these are the folks to which supervisors and managers devote an inordinate amount of their time.

The 80% in the middle are what I would consider reflective. They come to work and do what they are asked to do. I call them "reflective" because that is exactly what they're doing–they are "reflecting" on how the top 10% of their coworkers are treated and rewarded, and what steps are being taken to address the bottom 10% of their coworkers. If they notice that the top 10% are receiving no rewards/recognition/acknowledgement for their superior efforts, then they are probably thinking "why bother to excel?" If, on the other hand, they notice that absolutely nothing is being done with regard to the bottom 10% of their coworkers, then they are probably thinking "why not go that route, it's much easier?" Granted, personal pride will keep many of these "reflective" people from decidimg to become poor workers, but there will be some that will gravitate that way. More importantly, however, how many of these "reflective" people will fight the urge to excel when they can see no benefit in doing so, as evidenced by the "top 10% coworkers"?

It would appear then, that managers should make certain that they are addressing the needs of the top and bottom 10% groups, if they want to increase the chances of the "reflective" people gravitating toward, and ultimately becoming top performers.

ALLOCATION OF RESOURCES

Another aspect of organizing the unit is identifying your resource needs. One of the problems with determining the allocation of investigative personnel is the lack of specific study in this area. In other words, there aren't any charts out there that specify "if you have a police department with X number of personnel, you need X number of investigators." Although it would make things a whole lot simpler if such a chart existed, the process of determining just how many investigators an agency needs isn't really all that complicated.

There are basically two methods for determining manpower allocation for the investigative unit: the *traditional method* and the *manpower utilization method.*

I have a theory that goes like this: When I hear the term *traditional,* it probably should be called the "It Doesn't Really Work this way, and probably never will, but darn it, this is the way we've always done it and we're not going to change"method. When it comes to the traditional method of allocation of personnel for investigator units, my theory holds true. This method of determining personnel allocation is very simple: approximately 10–15% of the total sworn personnel of the police department are assigned to investigations. Neat, clean, and easy, but unfortunately often ineffective.

The manpower utilization method, on the other hand, is a little more complicated but infinitely more accurate. In this method, allocating personnel to the investigative unit is based on the actual work being done. It takes into account all of the tasks conducted by the unit and then allocates an adequate number of personnel to complete those tasks. This is actually a simple 6-step process. It requires no advanced mathematical calculations or formulas; it is based on simple logic and accurate information.

Step 1–The Total Number of Matters Assigned to the Investigation Unit on an Annual Basis is Tallied

This includes criminal cases assigned for follow-up investigation, background investigations on departmental employees, inquiries for persons seeking business licenses in the community, assists to other agencies in their investigations, and any other matters that the investigative unit is expected to handle. For this method to be successful, it is critically important that all of these matters are included. Anything assigned to the investigative unit must be counted to make this formula work. For the sake of our example, let's use a figure of 800 matters that are assigned to our mythical investigative unit over the course of a year.

Step 2—Multiply This Number by the Average Time it Takes to Complete an Assignment

You need to determine the average time required to complete these various matters over a specified period of time. It is easiest to use a six- or twelve-month period. Obviously, the only way you can determine these averages is with accurate records. Accurate record-keeping by the personnel performing these tasks is essential. Some of these matters, such as complex criminal investigations, might take weeks to complete, while other matters, such as a simple records check or an interview conducted to assist an outside agency, might take 30 minutes. Whatever the amount of time spent, it must be tallied, added together, and then divided by the number of matters addressed. Let's say you determine that the total time spent on all of the matters assigned to your investigative unit handled 200 assignments over the sample period and spent a total of 1,400 hours working those assignments. That number of hours, divided by the number of assignments, gives us the average time necessary to address a particular assignment.

1400 hours ÷ 200 assignments = 7 hours per assignment. Then, 7 hours x a projected 800 assignments = 5,600 total hours

Step 3—Administrative Time is Added to Cover Inspections, Equipment Maintenance, Training, Court Appearances, and Other Noninvestigative Duties

Investigators also spend time on noninvestigative duties, such as training, personnel and equipment inspections, and other assignments. When considering time for court appearances, be sure to include the time waiting to testify as well as the time participating in court proceedings. In order to be accurate, we must determine the total number of these hours spent by the investigative unit and factor this figure into our formula.

If we anticipate our investigators will devote a total of 400 hours of their time on these noninvestigative duties, we add that time to our running total.

400 hrs + 5,600 hrs = 6,000 hrs per year for investigative, administrative, and other duties

Step 4–Multiply This Figure by the Department's Assignment/ Availability Factor

Scheduling a 5-person shift for a 24-hour period would be easy if no one ever took a day off, sick day, vacation day, or training day.

Anyone who has ever been involved with scheduling knows that, in order to adequately schedule a 5-person shift, you need more than 5 people. You need to apply an assignment/availability factor, which takes into account these days off. The standard rule of thumb for this factor is 1.66. In other words, you actually need approximately one and two-thirds persons to perform the work of one person. Thus we need to factor that into our running total.

6,000 hours of total time x assignment availability factor of 1.66 = 9,960 total hours

Step 5–Divide This Figure by the Number of Hours in a Man-Year, Which is Approximately 2,080

The number of hours in a man-year is 2,080 hours, the result of multiplying 40 hours per week by 52 weeks (for a six-month data collection period, divide by 1,040 hours). We've already factored in the vacations, sick time, and so on. in Step 4, so we needn't duplicate that calculation. Note: if you're going to collect your activity data for a six-month period, when you get to this step, divide your final figure (in this example 9,960 hours) by one-half of a "man-year", or 1040 hours.

9,960 total hours ÷ 2,080 hours = 4.8*

---

*By this calculation, we would therefore need 4.8 (or roughly 5) investigators to complete the total amount of work.

Step 6–The Final Result is the Minimum Number of Investigators Required to Perform Investigative Duties

There are advantages to using the manpower utilization method. Without question, it is the most accurate method because the formula is based on the actual work done. The figures used in this formula are not concocted. They are accurate reflections of the work done by the unit.

As a chief of police, if I were approached by an investigative manager and asked to assign more personnel to the investigative unit, my first question would be "Why do you need them?" This would also be my first question if I were asked for more vehicles, more surveillance equipment, more cameras, more computers, or more anything. Considering that manpower is the most important and expensive resource in any law enforcement agency, the request should be based on sound data that clearly and legitimately justifies the need. I can guarantee you that if I approached the mayor or city council and asked for more officers, equipment, or funding, I would be asked the same question. This method is also the easiest to defend. As mentioned before, it is based on sound calculations and accurate data collection.

The Achilles' heel of this method is that it must be based on sound data. In order to accurately reflect the total number of hours expended on each case, recordkeeping must be accurate and complete. Inaccurate and/or incomplete timekeeping will make the calculations worthless. Keeping accurate records need not be difficult or too cumbersome. Since all cops hate needless paperwork, the importance of timekeeping must be carefully explained to them. If you are able to get across the idea that justification for more personnel will be based in large part on the actual work being done, as reflected by their timekeeping, the necessity of completing the timekeeping documents will sell itself.

If you use a timekeeping form, keep it as simple as possible. Fill in the blanks rather than narrative is the best format because this makes it more likely that the investigators will complete the form. You might also mandate that a copy of the time expenditure be attached to the final case report and reviewed prior to acceptance. This ensures that the amount of time actually spent investigating the case is reflected accurately. In order to accurately maintain this data, what is needed is a basic timekeeping form that includes the information necessary for the manpower allocation method. (See the example provided in Appendix 2.)

Chapter 5

RANK, POSITION, AND STATUS
OF INVESTIGATORS

The rank, status, and position of the investigator within the agency can have an impact on the operations of the investigative unit. In many agencies these matters are out of the hands of the investigative manager. Instead, they are determined by department policy, civil service regulations, collective bargaining agreements, or local or state laws. However, if you have input on these matters, there are some important issues you should take into account.

PERMANENT RANK

Some agencies have an actual rank of investigator or detective, which may be a permanent rank or position. Even if this issue is beyond your control, you must understand that the permanent rank of investigator can present some very serious problems. The Commission on Accreditation for Law Enforcement Agencies (CALEA) sets standards for member agencies and then carefully examines those agencies to determine their compliance with those standards. Many agencies at the state, county, and local levels have become accredited by CALEA. CALEA standards clearly state that *"Sworn positions in the criminal investigation component are the same as those used in the patrol component for rank titles or salary schedules, and that there should not be a unique set of ranks or rank structure within any operational component of the agency."*

In other words, CALEA feels that it should be possible to transfer personnel from the patrol force to the investigative unit (and vice versa) without regard for rank titles. The commission members oppose the permanent rank of investigator as they feel it limits the agency's ability to transfer personnel. The problems with establishing a permanent rank of investigator is that there is an implication, which can result in legal challenges, that the officer holding such a rank/position can only be removed for cause.

During a past command assignment, I was assigned as a district commander with responsibility for both patrol and investigations of a large agency. The investigative commander was having difficulties with a particular officer in his unit. This officer, who held a permanent investigative rank, presented a host of problems. He was unable to write even the simplest report in a competent and thorough manner, and his interviewing skills were terrible. He was lazy and often hard to locate, and these character traits were causing a great deal of disruption throughout the investigative unit. Additionally, this officer could not operate in an environment in which there was a great deal of freedom and autonomy. The investigative commander, a very bright and talented manager, approached me with the idea of returning the officer to a position in the patrol unit. Due to the permanent status of the officer's current investigative rank, this would involve a pay cut and, in fact, would be a demotion.

Fortunately, the commander had documented the many shortcomings of the officer. He had also collected a great deal of documentation from past performance evaluations and past supervisors that clearly showed these shortcomings had been going on for well over 10 years. I was wholeheartedly supportive of the commander's recommendation, as there were many deserving patrol officers who could have done a much better job in the position and whose backgrounds and work performance demonstrated that they could. In addition, it seemed that this officer had demonstrated that he was unable to function in a position that allowed as much freedom of movement and autonomy that was afforded to investigative personnel. In fact, this officer demonstrated for 10 years that he abused this freedom and autonomy at every opportunity. We began the process, only the second time this had been attempted. The first time someone was removed from the permanent investigative rank and returned to patrol it was determined on appeal that the transfer was "disciplinary in nature" and therefore contrary to the union contract. The decision was reversed, the officer was ordered back to investigations, and his rank was restored.

In this case, however, there was no pending disciplinary action, and we were able to clearly demonstrate that the officer did not possess even the basic skills to perform the tasks associated with the assignment. We were also able to demonstrate that whatever skills the officer did possess had not been used in performing the tasks. It seemed like a slam dunk situation, in which the officer would be back in a uniform in patrol by the end of the day. When the officer challenged the reassignment, the police union naturally took up his defense. After all, this would involve some loss, in the form of a salary decrease, to the officer. We were still confident in our position.

The process, which ended up before the state labor council in a long and protracted series of hearings, took a great deal of time and inconvenienced many people for months. The testimony was grueling, the hearing was long, and the attorneys were often difficult, but we were sure that we were doing the right thing for the unit and, more importantly, for the agency. We believed that this officer needed to be in a highly structured position where he would be more closely monitored. We also strongly felt that he had repeatedly demonstrated he did not possess the talents, skills, or abilities to continue as an investigator. The final decision contained both good news and bad news. The good news was that we had prevailed and the officer would be returning to the patrol assignment. The bad news was that the officer would retain the investigative rank and pay, and that the pay would be "red lined" until the pay of a patrol officer with the same seniority reached the same amount as this officer's current rate of pay. Upon his return to patrol, the officer demonstrated the same pathetic work ethic and was relegated to desk duty. For all I know, this officer is probably still there. This episode convinced me that the permanent rank or position of investigator is fraught with problems.

There are some additional problems associated with permanent rank of investigator:

- **It limits the opportunity, particularly in a smaller agency, to infuse new blood into the investigations unit.** In small to mid-sized agencies, there may only be a few officers assigned to investigations. In a department of 35 officers, for example, perhaps three or four might be assigned. If those three or four are given the permanent rank of investigator, there is virtually no way to infuse new blood into the investigative unit unless someone retires, is promoted, or dies. Assuming that all three or four of these personnel are hard-charging investigators with strong work ethics, this might not be a problem. But if they're not, it might be a major problem.

It has been my experience that the most difficult thing for a supervisor or chief of a small to mid-sized department to do is to keep things interesting for personnel. When the permanent rank of detective exists, this further limits the ability of the person in charge to move people around, infuse new blood, and keep it interesting.

- **It can stifle and/or frustrate ambitious and worthy patrol officers.** Giving patrol officers the opportunity to expand their horizons and learn new things can tremendously benefit not only the individual officer but the entire agency. The permanent rank of investigator takes away that opportunity, particularly if all of the personnel assigned to the investigative unit hold that rank.
- **It can create a false sense of permanent job status in less-than-stellar investigators.** This may be the most destructive and dangerous problem. The problem with this false sense of permanent job status is that it can sometimes cause these officers to not perform their tasks aggressively. In other words, they become R.I.P. (Retired in Place), where they are doing little more than taking up desk space. They do very little if any work and sometimes believe the only way that they could be removed involves using either a construction crane or a charge of dynamite. This is particularly destructive to an otherwise cohesive and hard-working unit. I have seen just one or two of these bad apples destroy a potentially good investigative unit.

PAY DIFFERENTIALS

Many agencies have some sort of pay differential for personnel assigned to the investigative unit. In some cases, the pay differential covers the cost of clothing the investigator must purchase for the assignment. This is particularly true in agencies that use the quartermaster method of providing uniforms and duty gear to patrol officers. In some agencies, differential is paid to compensate investigators for being required to be on call evenings, weekends, and holidays. Should a higher level of education/experience be required for assignment to the investigative unit, it may be only fair to pay a differential of some type. For example, if the patrol officer is required to only possess a high school diploma but investigators are required to possess a college degree, the pay differential might be linked to the more stringent educational requirement.

Sometimes these pay differentials are justified. It is important to note, however, that additional pay for investigators sometimes limits the agency's flexibility in transferring personnel. If the differential is viewed as a permanent part of the officer's salary and the officer is, for whatever reason, returned to an assignment without the differential, there may be a legal challenge to the resulting decrease in compensation. Once personnel become accustomed to receiving pay differentials, they often are reluctant to give them up.

As mentioned in the CALEA standard on ranks for investigators, equal pay for patrol officers and investigators facilitates lateral personnel movement without affecting an individual's income. Although this may be fundamentally true, I personally feel that if certain qualifying conditions are met, there need not be a problem with paying some type of differential to investigators. One of these conditions is that the reason for payment of the differential and the length of time that the differential will be paid must be *very clearly and carefully stated, preferably in writing.* If the differential is paid for the required business clothing or for being in an on-call status, this should be clearly stated and understood by both the agency and the investigator. Once the assignment as an investigator ends, so does the differential. As long as this is understood, it should not present a problem. The new investigator who has a problem with this arrangement has the option to not accept the assignment in the first place.

DUTY HOURS

In most agencies, particularly those with small or limited investigative units, working the day shift may be most practical for investigators. Working days gives investigators ready access to victims, witnesses, and businesspersons. The problem comes, however, when interviews and/or witness contact must take place after the normal day shift hours, which translates to overtime expenditures. Many agencies, even smaller agencies, schedule some investigators to work the afternoon shift. This allows for referrals for follow-up investigations by the afternoon patrol unit as well as for follow-up from investigations assigned to the day shift investigators. Problems sometimes arise in agencies that initiate an afternoon shift for investigators in that they neglect to build in enough turnover time to allow the dayshift and the afternoon shift investigators to discuss the ongoing investigations. If this is not done, duplication of effort, failure to conduct all necessary investigative steps, and a great deal of confusion can result. Shoddy investigative results are a distinct possibility.

Some agencies feel that time spent in this turnover briefing period is not necessary. They often attempt to address the issue with written briefing sheets intended to capture the work conducted by the day shift in enough detail to allow the afternoon shift to hit the ground running on the investigations. The problem with briefing sheets is that paper reports don't carry all of the nuances of the investigative effort and don't allow for questions by the oncoming shift. Even if it is only a 30-minute turnover briefing, it is time well spent, and it will go a long way in ensuring that consistency and thoroughness are a part of the investigative efforts of both shifts.

For most small to mid-sized agencies, there is usually no need to assign investigators to the midnight shift. Well-trained patrol officers conducting full-scale preliminary investigations usually make it unnecessary for an investigator to sit in the station by the phone all night waiting for an assignment.

CALL-OUT STATUS

The commanders of the investigations and the patrol divisions, with the agreement of the chief, should specify the circumstances under which investigators must respond to crimes that occur after regular investigative unit duty hours and appear to need their immediate attention. This should be done in writing; an example of a policy showing these responsibilities was presented in Chapter 1. The sample policy shown in Appendix 1 specifies that the patrol unit is responsible for preliminary investigations into all offenses and further specifies when the preliminary investigation ends and the follow-up investigation begins. Having such a document in an agency's operations manual, and making certain that supervisors and managers in both the patrol unit and the investigative unit are familiar with the policy, will help avoid the squabbles and misunderstandings that often arise when call-outs are made prematurely, not made properly, or not made at all.

Even though a comprehensive policy might exist, however, having investigators on a standby status (which usually refers to time periods including the midnight shift during the week, weekends, and holidays) is usually a necessary part of the management of the investigative unit. Standby status may also imply restriction of movement, such as prohibition from leaving home, leaving the community, or some other type of restriction.

There is usually some type of benefit provided to the investigator on standby. Some agencies provide a certain amount of overtime pay or compensatory time off for completing the standby period: for example, "for each 8-hour time period the investigator completes on standby status, they will receive one hour of overtime," or something similar. Most union contracts guarantee some type of compensation. Investigators who are required to wear and respond to pagers or cell phones are usually included in these provisions.

When considering the question of a call-out status for investigators, your primary concern must be fairness. Among investigators who are specialists, the on-call status might be limited to requests for assistance involving whatever their particular specialty might be. In a unit made up of general assignment investigators, however, a simple rotation might be easiest. Placing a investigator on standby from Monday morning at 8 a.m. until the following Monday morning at 8 a.m. means that the investigator is responsible for responding to requests for investigative assistance each weekday evening, any holidays that fall during the week, and all weekend. It may not be advisable to have a system whereby any cases for which the investigator is called out are automatically assigned to that investigator. An investigator who is on standby status during a particularly active time period in which a great deal of crime occurs may very well end up with an excessive caseload. It might be better to have the on-call investigator conduct the initial follow-up investigation and then you can assign the case to another investigator, taking caseload and other considerations into account.

Chapter 6

SELECTING INVESTIGATIVE PERSONNEL

Selecting the best available personnel to function as investigators can have a tremendous bearing on the success of their investigations, which will, in turn, obviously have an impact on the overall success of the investigative unit. Your likely pool of candidates for an investigator position will consist of patrol officers, so the first step in making your selection is to understand how the two roles differ: While patrol officers usually expend most of their efforts on *maintaining order and providing general services to the public,* investigators specialize in activities primarily related to *law enforcement.*

DESIRABLE QUALITIES FOR INVESTIGATORS

There are certain qualities you should consider when selecting investigators. These include:

• Talent in gathering information
• Talent in field operations
• Conviction rates
• Personnel record.

Talent in Gathering Information

There is no question that the ability to gather information is a prerequisite for success as an investigator, but information comes from a variety of sources. To be successful, the investigator must be able to gather this information from any source. Crime scenes are a major source of information, and proper scene management is one area you should examine when determining the applicant's ability to gather information. An officer's ability to successfully manage crime scenes should include:

• Protecting the scene itself for potential physical evidence
• Managing potential witnesses at or near the scene
• Handling of the victim(s) at the scene or at medical facilities.

You need to carefully examine all of the officers' communications skills. To that end, there are several questions you should ask yourself, such as:

• Can the officer verbally communicate in an effective manner?
• Can listeners quickly determine what message the officer is giving?
• Do listeners willingly provide information to the officer?
• If required, can the officer conduct successful interviews with witnesses, victims, and others?

These elements are particularly important and predictive of the future success of the officer as an investigator. The success of interviews often depends on the verbal communication skills of the investigator and can be affected by the display of genuine sensitivity and concern throughout the evidence-gathering process.

In addition to verbal communications, is the officer capable of preparing professional reports? In most law enforcement agencies, the reports prepared by patrol officers consist of a fill-in-the-blank front side and a short narrative back side. The format of reports completed by most investigators, on the other hand, is generally completely narrative. This means all potential investigators must be able to communicate via written reports in a manner that reflects their potential to utilize narrative reporting. Many studies have shown that favorable outcomes of investigations depend on investigators preparing legible, concise, accurate, comprehensible, and complete reports. Prosecutors use written reports to gain convictions, and the investigator who is not capable of preparing concise, legible, complete reports is not much use in the prosecutorial phase.

Talent in Field Operations

This is demonstrated in an officer's proven ability in patrol techniques and street knowledge. Is the officer capable of conducting activities such as stakeouts, where participants are expected to remain in a specific location for an extended period of time? Stamina and willingness to work long hours are also important attributes for conducting field operations. Unlike patrol, investigations is not always an 8-hour-a-day job. Investigators often are required to continue working as investigative leads come in, often for long periods of time, particularly in major cases.

Another question to ask is whether the officer handles themselves effectively on the street. Can they recognize a crime pattern in an area, or do they require that this information be provided to them? Can they effectively deal with the criminal element as well as legitimate citizens, or does the criminal element easily take advantage of them? This is often referred to as being street-smart, and it is a difficult trait to define. Although it is true that most patrol officers have limited contact with actual hard-core criminals, the patrol officer should be able to interact with criminals without repeatedly being conned. Most patrol officers pick this up naturally with some time on the job, but some patrol officers never seem to get it.

Conviction Rates

Arrests, prosecutions, convictions, and conviction rates should be carefully examined. Care must be taken, however, to look at not just the *quantity* but also the *quality* of arrests. The number of arrests alone is often not an accurate indicator of an officer's effectiveness. If the number of arrests is the only thing you consider, the officer who is capable of successfully handling a situation that does not require an arrest doesn't get credit for doing so. There are many situations when not making an arrest and taking an alternative course of action is wiser, such as successfully defusing some volatile situations. Officers who are capable of discerning these situations and properly addressing them should be recognized for their efforts. When arrest rates are counted without regard to quality, officers who take wiser actions are in effect penalized. The number of arrests actually reflects the *quantitative dimension*; the conviction rate reflects the *qualitative dimension*. A recent study conducted for the Institute for Law and Social Research revealed that conviction rate, when properly monitored and measured, was a useful measure for assessing the performance of police. There is a simple formula to illustrate the concept of conviction rate:

$$Conviction\ Rate = \frac{Arrests\ Ending\ in\ Conviction}{Total\ Arrests}$$

For example, if an officer makes 200 arrests, and 100 of those arrests result in convictions, the conviction rate would be 50%. One must take into account that these convictions might not necessarily be for the original offense charged, as plea bargaining and pleas to lesser included offenses are common. Although not all arrests result in conviction, measured this way the conviction rate is often a measure of an officer's awareness of his or her responsibility for preparing cases against arrestees so they can be successfully prosecuted and for not making unwarranted arrests. Officers who do not make unnecessary arrests are therefore not penalized when determining their overall efficiency.

The study, which encompassed 7 agencies and 10,200 officers, found that 19% of the officers examined in Los Angeles accounted for over 50% of the arrests that ended in conviction. In Manhattan, 8% of the officers made 50% of the arrests resulting in conviction. Overall, 12% of the 10,200 officers studied were responsible for more than half of all convictions, while 22% effected not a single arrest that ended in conviction during the study period. The study also identified several other factors worth mentioning:

- Officers with high conviction rates responded more rapidly to calls for service, managed more effectively at crime scenes, and were more adept at locating, questioning, and managing witnesses.
- Officers with high conviction rates exerted substantial effort to pursue, recover, and preserve tangible evidence at the scene, searched the surrounding area, and followed up on all leads.
- Officers with high conviction rates conducted thorough neighborhood canvasses and expended more effort to locate witnesses.
- Officers with high conviction rates displayed superior techniques of interviewing and interrogation, asking questions directly related to the investigation rather than psychological techniques (which rarely work anyway).

The point is simple. When selecting investigators, the *conviction rate* of the patrol officer, not just the *raw number of arrests made*, should be considered.

Personnel Records

Another element you should consider when selecting investigators is an examination of the *objective data found in the officer's personnel records.* By objective data, I mean observable, measurable data that is not based on someone's subjective interpretation. The information sought should relate to the officer's daily professional work behavior essential for effective performance as an investigator. Items such as absenteeism, use of sick time, valid complaints against the officer, and awards received are indicators of typical behaviors. Items such as punctuality, safe driving, courteousness, relying only on necessary force, restraint in using weapons, physical fitness, and the ability to get along with others are character traits essential to success as an investigator. Investigator selection should use carefully examined, objective data. If a patrol officer can't make it to work on time, is the subject of a disproportionate number of complaints, and abuses sick time, all of which are objective data, what do you think you'd have if this officer were selected for a position as an investigator? You'll have an investigator who can't make it to work on time, is the subject of a disproportionate number of complaints, and abuses sick time. *The only difference is that the investigator will be doing these things in plainclothes, not in a uniform.*

With regard to disciplinary action, I believe that misconduct on previous assignments is often predictive of later disciplinary complaints. Officers who can't seem to do their job without receiving (valid) complaints from the public, other agencies or other officers probably won't fare much better if assigned as investigators. In addition, subjective data, such as supervisory performance evaluations, should also be examined. Do not, however, take these evaluations at face value. Personal biases, unfair evaluations, favoritism, and other subjective flaws can detract from the accuracy of performance evaluations.

Evaluation instruments that examine traits such as motivation, stability, street knowledge, persistence, intelligence, judgment, teamwork, reliability, and dedication are the most valuable. Of all of these dimensions, *motivation* is the best predictor of success in investigations. Can the officer motivate themselves to conduct proactive enforcement efforts, or do they need to be "led by the hand"? It has been my observation that self-motivated officers are interested in and take pride in their work, make the extra effort to solve crimes, and tend to derive satisfaction from doing their best.

Other Qualifications

Some agencies have additional *mandatory qualifications* for officers seeking investigator positions, such as time on the job or completion of college credit or other training programs. Some agencies use written examinations as part of the investigator selection process. My only concern with written examinations is if they are used as the *sole determinant* of the selection process, the agency is likely missing out on a great deal of information that, in my opinion, would better predict success as an investigator. Rarely can written exams successfully predict arrest activity and investigative skills, including evidence gathering and crime scene management, behaviors crucial to success as an investigator. In addition, written examinations sometimes reflect nothing more than the ability of the officer to absorb information for a short period of time and regurgitate it during a written exam. In other words, just because someone is a good test-taker doesn't mean that they'll necessarily be a good investigator. With these things in mind, however, there are some very good examinations available. If exams are given, thought should be given to providing a reading list to allow candidates to prepare, which in and of itself will provide an indicator of how badly they want the investigative assignment and how willing they are to prepare themselves.

Another trait you should consider is the verbal ability of the officer. The ability to successfully communicate, particularly under pressure, is something else that can predict future success as an investigator. This ability is without question a trait crucial to the investigative role. Using interviews as part of the selection process, as long as the interview is not the sole determinant, is something that you should consider. There is no question that some officers are experts at taking written examinations but might not otherwise be very talented. It is also true that some officers appear very talented during an oral interview when there isn't really a great deal of real talent there.

As you can see, selecting the most suitable officers for investigative positions will definitely impact the success of the unit. This is why the selection strategy you use should be as thorough as the selection strategy for new patrol officers. The next section deals with selecting new investigators.

INVESTIGATOR SELECTION STRATEGIES

When selecting investigators, the agency should use a selection strategy that best suits their needs. Unfortunately, few, if any, written materials or rules about selecting investigators exist. In some agencies, personnel are promoted to investigator to reward nearly any form of behavior, accomplishment, or special service that the top department management wants to encourage. Obviously, care must be taken that the main desire for the investigative assignment isn't the desire for more freedom and a less-structured work environment. Other agencies sometimes use involvement in a shooting as a precursor to becoming an investigator. Although I have nothing but the utmost respect for any police officer who survives a shootout, this should not be the sole determining factor for investigator selection.

Some agencies are restricted in the selection strategy they use. Collective bargaining agreements may be in place that dictate which officers will become investigators, usually based on seniority to some extent. There are some definite disadvantages to selecting investigators strictly by seniority, and I feel management should strenuously resist this type of arrangement, if sought by a labor union. The investigator position is too important to be given automatically to someone based on seniority. In these situations, I strongly recommend the process of temporary or rotating investigative positions be at least considered for some of the positions in the investigative unit. This process is examined in Chapter 6.

Regardless of the selection strategy you use, there is one problem you should avoid. If you already know who you want to select and are merely going through the motions to make it look like your agency is fair, professional, or open-minded, don't waste your time. A charade leads to a complete loss of credibility. This loss of credibility doesn't just apply to the investigator selection process but to every other process or decision made in the future. Cops are the hardest people in the world to con, because we're so suspicious. Once cops know someone is trying to con or lie to them, *nothing* that person ever says in the future will be believed.

I once helped a friend prepare for his department's promotional process for sergeant by reviewing a videotape he had received from his last attempt. The interview consisted of a series of questions asked by a firm doing an assessment center-type exercise. None of the candidates (supposedly) had any advance knowledge of the questions used for the interview. In the videotape, one of the department's command officers could be seen entering and leaving the room during the interview portion. I asked my friend if this command officer had been involved in the process as an assessor, to which he replied no. I then asked if there were any other candidates waiting in the wings for their interviews. He told me only one, and that the other candidate happened to be the best friend of the command officer who had been repeatedly entering and leaving the room. Guess who got the position? Guess who was the best prepared and gave the best interview?

This illustration brings up two very important points. The first goes toward the integrity of the firm conducting the process, which is questionable at best. The second, more important question goes to the credibility of the agency conducting the process. Once either is lost they cannot be recovered. So don't open yourself up to controversy. Simply select the officer that you are going to select in the end anyway and avoid the charade. Don't think that you're fooling any of the other officers with the process, because you're not.

Although there are no textbooks that provide a step-by-step process to select investigators, there are some common selection strategies or styles that agencies use.

Unstructured Style

Sometimes selecting investigators is based on undefined and completely discretionary factors, which are subject to frequent change and interpretation. I remember asking two command officers at a previous assignment how investigators were selected. The laughing reply included the fact that one of the investigators had been a drinking buddy of the former chief, another was a fishing and golfing friend of the investigative commander, and yet another was the husband of a good friend of the chief's wife. This is not to say that the ability to fish or golf is necessarily a bad thing, but these traits should not be part of the selection process. The unstructured style usually includes key factors that sound good but are often nebulous such as previous experience and quality of work. What does this mean? It means whatever the person using it as a selection criteria *wants it to mean.*

In the unstructured style, if you examine personnel records, there are typically no rules on how you should apply these records to the selection process. I recall one agency that, to appear legitimate during an investigator selection process, wrote a job description that required the person selected to have completed certain schools, have a minimum number of years on the job, and be a certified range officer. The one and only candidate who possessed these qualifications was the one and only candidate they wanted to select in the first place. How transparent!

Semi-Structured Style

In this style, which lies midway between the unstructured and the structured styles, there may be defined and formalized general procedures, but there is also substantial latitude in the application of these procedures. In other words, the weight given to each part of the process is based on who is carrying out the assessment. This style usually involves some type of a minimum performance evaluation mark and requires the recommendation of the officer's current immediate supervisor. Personnel may be subject to interviews, but the questions used and the interviews themselves are sometimes inconsistent. There may be some examination of objective data in personnel files, but the weight given to the data as they relate to the overall process is inconsistent. Similar to the unstructured style, the semi-structured style falls into the grey area of not appearing legitimate. For that reason you should probably avoid it.

Structured Style

In this style, the entire process is defined in writing, including the rules, requirements, and any procedures that will be used. Little discretion is allowed in the process, which involves some type of objective scoring and the establishment of eligibility lists at the conclusion of the process. If your promotional process is mandated by a civil service system, you may have virtually no discretion. There are very firm rules on applications, publication of openings, testing, and all other aspects of the process.

In a structured style, items such as peer evaluations, staff evaluations, and interviews are often used, and the weight given to these items is clearly stated beforehand. In addition, sometimes outside assessors are used, which can go a long way to add credibility to the entire process. Some type of a structured selection strategy helps you identify the most suitable personnel for investigative positions. Although it takes a little more time and is more work, it has some definite advantages. First, it is a legitimate process. Selections are based on what you are capable of doing rather than who you know. Second, a structured strategy is good for agency morale. When cops don't believe they've gotten a fair chance at something, it's difficult for them to accept or believe *anything* agency administrators tell them. Clearly a structured style is best. The process presented next follows that strategy.

A STRUCTURED SELECTION PROCESS

What follows is an example of a thorough, fair, complete, and defensible selection process. The elements of the process are designed to evaluate the abilities and potential of the applicant in a variety of areas that can predict success as an investigator. There are several forms and procedures that can be used in a structured selection process. (See the example provided in Appendix 3.)

Position Announcement

All personnel must receive the announcement regarding open investigator positions at the same time; this precludes the impression of favoritism or predisposition to notify only selected personnel. I recommend that the announcement be made verbally at all roll calls and briefings and in writing to all patrol officers, both individually in their mail as well as on bulletin boards. This way, nobody can say that they weren't aware of the openings. The announcement should list as much information as possible as to the position description for investigator, including a short summary of the duties, hours of work, location of assignment, and any specifics regarding the assignment (i.e., bilingual ability prerequisites, undercover work, etc.). In addition, the announcement should clearly state the dates the selection process will commence, when the interviews and other parts of the process will be held, and when selection is anticipated.

You should also publish a timetable with the announcement, including the following elements:

- **Announcement date.** Date when the announcement goes out to all eligible candidates
- **Application deadline.** Allow enough time for you to advertise the position and for candidates to fill out applications
- **Selection deadline.** Make this date known to eligible candidates.

Candidate Application

You should use a standardized application form. Simply asking for resumes from personnel is not the best way to gather the information. Personnel should have their qualifications assessed by their experience, education, and training, not by how professional their resume appears. A standardized application form will level the playing field and allow all personnel to start from the same point. The sample application form that follows allows for the candidate to highlight the following information:

- Law enforcement experience with their current police department and any other experience
- Investigative experience with their current police department and any other experience
- Any investigative training they have completed
- A commentary regarding what the officer considers to be his or her two best investigations while assigned to a patrol function. (Copies of both field reports are required to be submitted with the form.)

- Any special skills the officer possesses that they feel would aid him or her as an investigator.

In order to obtain this information in a standardized format that allows all applicants to initiate the process from a level playing field, a standardized form should be used. (See the example provided in Appendix 4.)

Candidate Interview

I recommend that the interview be conducted by a panel of investigative supervisors, and strongly suggest you consider using outside agency personnel. The use of outside agency personnel in the investigator selection process adds a great deal of credibility to the entire process, and removes the idea of favoritism or predisposition to select certain personnel. This might cost no more than the price of lunch for the panelists. The panel, before the interview, will receive each candidate's application, including the case reports that they have submitted to accompany their application. The application is provided to panelists only to familiarize them with the candidates, and it will not be scored until after the interview. This is done to preclude the panelist from having preconceived notions about the candidate during the interview, which could impact the scoring of the interview portion.

As stated, when the candidate submits his or her application, they are required to attach copies of what they consider to be their two best investigations, which can be preliminary investigative reports. After the applications are received, obtain two additional, random field reports the applicant has completed. These reports may be more indicative of the candidate's *daily* performance and are more likely to reflect accurately the manner in which the candidate typically completes reports. I would also recommend that the candidate be given a time for the interview in writing and told (in writing) to report no later than 15 minutes before the interview. The reason for the 15 minutes is that when the candidate reports for the interview he or she will be given a criminal case scenario to review and told to be prepared to discuss the scenario at the interview. The candidate should use the time before the interview to review the case and decide on a course of action. This will induce some stress on the candidate. And of course, if the candidate arrives less than 15 minutes before the interview they have less time to prepare, which can induce even more stress. Using the case scenario also helps you determine if they can follow directions by arriving when instructed to do so. I recall one situation in which the candidate, told in writing to arrive 15 minutes before the time scheduled for his interview, arrived 2 minutes before the start of the interview. He was handed the case scenario, and about 30 seconds later (hardly enough time to read it and formulate a plan) he was ushered in to his interview.

At the scheduled time the candidate is called before the panel. The first part of the interview is a review of the application packet submitted by the candidate. Panelists have reviewed the packet beforehand and may have questions or request clarification regarding training and background. The case reports submitted by the candidate are discussed. Following this review of the application packet, the standardized interview questions are covered. After the interview, the candidate will then be asked to present his or her course of action regarding the criminal case scenario. Asking the candidate to present his case review *after* the application review and interview should provide the panel some idea as to how the candidate functions when his thought process is interrupted and how well the candidate can think on his feet. Many candidates will assume that the case scenario will be the first thing discussed.

The candidate interview, conducted by the panel, consists of standardized questions. Panelists will refrain from adding their own questions or modifying the questions provided to them. It is recommended that the questions be asked in a round-robin style, with the same panelist being responsible for the same questions for each of the candidates. The following are some suggested questions you might use. You will also find a sample form for this at the back of the book.

1. **Why do you want to be an investigator?** This standard question can give insight into some of the real reasons the candidate wants the investigative assignment. If the answer provided has anything to do with getting out of the uniform or getting away from changing shifts, that candidate should be very closely scrutinized.

2. **What do you see as the daily activities of an investigator?** This question can serve as a reality check to see if the candidate

has any real idea what investigators actually do on a day-to-day basis. In the event that the job description and typical duties of the investigator have appeared in the announcement for the position, the answer provided by the candidate might also reflect their reading and comprehension skills.

3. **What do you feel should be the criteria for selection of an investigator?** This question can provide an idea of what skills the candidate feels are needed to fulfill the duties of an investigator.

4. **What are your strongest attributes that would make you an effective investigator?** This is another method of seeing how realistic the candidate is as well as determining if they actually understand the duties they would be expected to perform. If the candidate is unable to sell themselves to a selection panel, how could they be expected to sell themselves to a suspect in order to gain his or her cooperation?

5. **What skills do you feel you need to improve on to make you a better police officer?** This is another way of asking someone their weak points, but can also point to their desire for further training and to what they envision their future to be within the agency.

It should be noted that there are many questions that routinely come up and are asked at investigator selection interviews that are not only totally inappropriate but border on the illegal. For example, asking a female officer if the fact that she has young children would hamper her ability to respond to call-outs is totally inappropriate, unless every other officer (males included) is asked the same question. The easiest way to avoid asking inappropriate questions is to have the same panelist ask the same question(s) for each candidate, and to insist that the panelist read the question verbatim. Each of these questions should be rated on a scale of one to three (one being a weak answer and three being a strong one) by each interviewer. Each interviewer totals their ratings and the five ratings are added together to give a composite rating of the candidate's interview.

Before the interview process, the panelists have received both the case scenario and suggested basic investigative steps that the candidate should be able to verbalize in his or her presentation. The candidate's case scenario presentation should be critiqued based on the following criteria:

1. Thoroughness of their review of the scenario
2. Logical sequence of their proposed investigative steps
3. Knowledge of the law regarding the crimes involved in the scenario
4. Knowledge of evidentiary value and procedures
5. Creativity of their proposed investigative efforts
6. Strengths and weaknesses of their proposal
7. Thoroughness of the proposed investigative steps.

Each of these criteria should be rated on a scale of one to three (again, one being a weak answer and three being a strong one) by each interviewer. Again, interviewers total their scores and the scores are added together to give a composite rating of the case scenario.

In addition to the application packet, interview questions, and case scenario, it is beneficial for each candidate to be scored by panelists on the following criteria that are indicative of professional conduct:

1. Punctuality
2. Professional appearance and demeanor
3. Verbal communication skills
4. Ability to follow directions.

The question of the candidate's ability to follow directions can be evaluated by many facets of their participation in the selection process. I was on a selection panel for a large agency once and, while on a break from the interviews, saw a young patrol officer I knew walking into the building. The requirements for the position of investigator with this particular agency were that the candidate must have completed two years of college credit. At that time, candidates for entry-level patrol officer needed a high school diploma. As I approached my friend the patrol officer, I remarked that I wasn't aware that he had re-enrolled and finished his college classes. He told me that he hadn't, but thought that he'd apply and come to the interview anyway because he felt that by being bilingual it would somehow grant him a waiver of the college credit requirement. The notice for the qualifications happened to be posted on a nearby bulletin board. I drew his attention to the notice, asking if he saw anything on the notice that would support his theory regarding his receiving a waiver for being bilingual. He said no, and I told him that he had to make a choice. He could either go into the interview and confirm for all of the panelists that he was incapable of following directions, which would no doubt irritate all of us for wasting our time; or go to the secretary assigning the preinterview case scenarios and withdraw his name from consideration. Fortunately, he chose to save himself the embarrassment and withdrew his name. Although this may sound harsh or uncaring, if he couldn't follow simple directions for a position he wanted, how could he be expected to follow directions on a serious investigation?

Each of the following criteria should be rated on a scale of 1 to 3 (1 being low and 3 being high) by each panelist. Each interviewer should total his or her ratings and the ratings will be added together to give a composite rating of the candidate's interview: (See the example provided in Appendix 5.)

- Interview questions
- Criminal case scenario
- Application packet
- Professional skills.

The result will be a combined score for each candidate. This score will include the composite score of the following elements in the process:

- Composite rating of interview questions
- Composite rating of criminal case scenario
- Composite rating of application packet
- Composite rating of professional conduct criteria.

These scores are totaled and the result is the overall score for each candidate. Although it might appear that this process is cumbersome and takes a great deal of time, each time I have used it I have judged the overall success of the process on one factor. When the interviews were conducted and the eligibility list and/or selections were completed, I surveyed all of the candidates who were not selected. I have yet to receive a negative comment on the process itself. On the contrary, even the most disappointed candidates have indicated that, in their opinion, the process itself was very fair. That to me is a ringing endorsement of the process, when even the unsuccessful candidates believed that they received a fair shake.

What Happens if Nobody Applies?

With all of the various elements and strategies for selecting investigators taken into account, what happens if you advertise the openings for investigator positions and nobody applies?

There can be a number of reasons why there wouldn't be applicants for the position of investigator, which can include:

- **Financial considerations**- in many agencies there is a greater opportunity for overtime compensation for patrol personnel rather than investigators. I am familiar with several union contracts that dictate that if there is an "open shift" due to illness, on-duty injury, or expanded duties, that the opportunity to work those open shifts goes first to personnel assigned to patrol duties. In addition, the fact that patrol works basically a fixed number of hours in a day allows for more opportunity for "side jobs" or secondary employment. Many police personnel depend on this secondary income for the comfort of their families, and anything that would preclude them from working it, such as the often irregular hours routinely worked by investigators is often not seen as desirable.
- **Irregular scheduling**- many police personnel want to know exactly when they are working months in advance. With patrol schedules this is possible, but with the schedules of investigators, coupled with the "call-out" or standby situations, in which they are mandated to miss out on family and other personal events, it is usually not as definite. The distinct likelihood of having to miss such things as weddings, graduations, and other "life events" due to working long hours on an investigation just doesn't appeal to some people.
- **Inability to attend school**- due to the competitive nature of the law enforcement profession, many police personnel have returned to college, graduate school, law school, or other academic pursuits. While this is laudable, being assigned to an investigative position makes furthering one's education much more difficult. Many people see the attainment of higher educational pursuits as something that will benefit them, not only during, but after their police career, and they are unlikely to seek a position that might preclude them from that goal. While many colleges and universi-

ties offer "shift-friendly" scheduling for public safety personnel, which can include "mirrored classes," in which the same classes are conducted during both during days and evenings. The hours that some investigators are expected to work will usually not fit into even "shift-friendly" scheduling.

The "downside" is that these concerns are realistic and may preclude some officers from applying for investigative positions, while the "upside" is that personnel who do apply for investigative positions usually are doing so in spite of these restrictions to their lives. That means in many cases that they are applying to become investigators for all the right reasons—their goal is to see cases through to their conclusion and improve the chances that justice will be served.

Some of the methods for combating the lack of interest in the position can include rotational or temporary investigative assignments, which will be discussed in detail in Chapter 6. In addition, the concept of "recruitment" is something that should be considered. If there is a particularly talented patrol officer who has demonstrated the types of skills that would suit them well for an investigative assignment there is absolutely nothing wrong with "recruiting" them to apply for an investigative opening. Of course, professional courtesy dictates that you advise their supervisor of your "recruitment" efforts. Over the years I have targeted several sharp patrol officers and encouraged them to apply for a variety of assignments, to include investigative positions and several specialty positions. I've always viewed this "recruitment" as part of the "succession planning" that all good managers are supposed to perform. Succession planning means that although we'd all like to consider ourselves completely irreplaceable, we're not, and when those of us in management positions leave, our organizations and our profession must go on without us. Without succession planning, organizations stagnate and performance decreases. Looking for talented personnel and encouraging them to apply for positions that will allow them to utilize their skills and talents and really "grow" is good management.

In addition to the personal restrictions that the investigative assignment can place on the life of an investigator and their family, the investigative manager who is in a situation where nobody wants to apply for investigative openings should also take a very hard look at the overall morale of the agency. In situations where poor morale exists, there is often a dramatic decrease in the number of personnel who want to apply for anything.

When considering the morale of an agency, I have noted several situations over the years that I consider indicators of morale. This is not to say that if one of these situations is occurring that the morale of an agency has hit "rock bottom," but the organizations that I have observed with the worst morale usually had more than a couple of the following occurring:

- **Sick Time Abuse**–when people have very low morale, work is truly the last place that they want to be, and in these cases, even a bout with "the sniffles" can take on major implications. This is particularly true in agencies with liberal sick time policies, in which there is really nothing lost if the officer takes off sick.

- **Chargeable Accidents or Personal Injuries**–when people have very low morale, they are not paying adequate attention to what they're doing, and this is particularly true when operating motor vehicles or when considering the safety aspects of their jobs. While a certain number of accidents or injuries are bound to occur in any agency, an inordinate number of accidents or injuries by an individual officer or agency-wide is not acceptable.

- **Tardiness**–when people have very low morale, they want to spend as little time as is humanly possible at the source of their discomfort, which is work. They will breeze into their "roll call" briefing one minute before their shift starts and will leave within one minute after the shift ends. Excessive tardiness is an indicator that the morale is so low that these individuals don't even care enough to attempt to get to work on time.

- **Sustained Citizen Complaints**–when people have very low morale, they sometimes have a tendency to infuse their feelings of unhappiness into their everyday jobs. This can result in their being impolite or disrespectful to the public, probably based on the "I'm miserable, so why should you be anything better" theory. Unfortunately, this can also manifest itself in worse ways, to include legitimate excessive force complaints. Of course, in any agency there will be a number (hopefully small) of citizen complaints, but if there are an excessive number or a significant "spike" in the number of complaints, morale should be considered.

- **Excessive Number of Grievances**–in organizations with very low morale, the day-to-day situations that are usually "shrugged off" become major incidents, which often results in grievances for organizations with collective bargaining agreements. Many of these grievances filed in organizations with very low morale are not really focused on significant incidents or policies, but are more of the "nuisance" variety, just filed to irritate management. I suppose that this is probably also based on the "I'm miserable, so why should you be anything better" theory.

Although this is not a book on maintaining good morale in a police organization, I feel that it is among the most important responsibilities of anyone in management to see to it that good morale is established and maintained. There are two other things to ask yourself if you even suspect that the morale of your agency is slipping or has slipped, and these are:

1. The last time you gave a promotional examination, what percentage of the eligible personnel took the examination? In agencies with very low morale, many people will forego the opportunity for advancement and more money because they see the administration of the agency to be a large part of the problem and frankly don't want to be a part of the problem.
2. The second question to ask is how many times does the communications center have to assign a backup patrol officer on a call vs. officers jumping in to back each other up without being assigned to do so. In organizations with very good morale, it has been my experience that rarely if ever does the communications center have to assign any backup officers–the personnel care enough about each other's safety to do it on their own. In organizations with very low morale, personnel oftentimes don't want to be bothered–they want to complete their shift, go home, and be left alone.

Chapter 7

DEVELOPING NEW INVESTIGATORS

Following an intensive selection process, you will need to spend time developing a new investigator. A development process will likely include formal and informal training as well as temporary or rotational assignments. Investigative managers often say they don't have the time or money available to allow for this process. It can be costly to implement a full development process, but it can be even costlier not to.

TRAINING

The development of a new investigator begins with formal training. Many investigative managers are so short-handed that when they receive a new investigator they immediately want to get them assigned to cases and working. Unfortunately, although this tactic might save you some time when the investigator is new, it usually costs you more time down the road. The investigator often learns their lessons the hard way, by making mistakes. You then have to devote time to going back and training the investigator in what he or she should have been taught in the first place. For many agencies, training means that old standby, OJT (on-the-job training). OJT might work for an officer assigned on a temporary basis, such as a 60–90 day program. I strongly recommend, however, against using that method for investigators either assigned permanently or on a long-term rotational basis. When you consider that the new patrol officer receives (depending on state statutes or agency policy) from two months to a year of academy training, it only stands to reason that someone moving from a patrol officer position to an investigator assignment should have *some* formal training. Although I don't believe this requires several months of investigator academy, I do strongly advocate some form of formal training.

Benefits of Formal Training

There are a number of benefits to an investigator training program. First of all, *formal training increases competence.* Many functions of the investigator position will be totally new to the newly assigned investigator. Realistically, how many patrol officers are involved in intensive interrogations on criminal suspects? How many are adept at putting together applications for search warrants? How many have ever had to cultivate and utilize a confidential source of information? How many have had to conduct a moving or stationary surveillance? When you get down to it, the basic question regarding new investigator training is whether these new tasks should be learned correctly through a formal training program or through OJT, which is often a hit-or-miss proposition. It isn't acceptable to allow someone to fail, and then to use that failure to teach them the correct way to perform the task. By not exposing the new investigator to some formal training, you run that risk.

Second, *formal training assures that the transition from patrol officer to investigator is made, not just on paper, but where it really counts: in the mind of the officer.* Although there are many similarities between the job of the patrol officer and the job of the investigator, there are many different demands made on an investigator, and training can help meet those demands. To ask an officer to rise to these demands and be successful is much easier if, in the mind of the officer, he or she is actually qualified to be in the position. The goal is to instill in the mind of the officer that they are now something more than a patrol officer. They are now a specialist, trained and ready to overcome any difficulties that they might encounter in the assignment. Basic investigative training, augmented by specialized investigative training, gives them confidence and increases their potential for success in the new assignment.

It is common for the investigative manager, who may have been working short-handed until the arrival of the new investigator, to fall into the trap of "I'm so short-handed that I can't afford to lose a resource for the time it takes to complete the formal training program." Actually, you can't afford not to considering how quickly the field of criminal investigations changes. Once initial training is completed, updates must be offered to cover changes in laws, new techniques, and so on. An example is the surge in identity theft offenses. In order to be able to successfully investigate these offenses, formal training is essential.

Third, *training increases the new investigator's morale.* Going into a completely new assignment can be traumatic for anybody, particularly going into an investigative assignment. Most investigators I know take great (some might even say perverse) pleasure in giving the new investigator as much grief as is humanly possible. Focusing on each and every mistake the new investigator makes is a way of gathering ammunition for yet another assault of humor, always at the expense of the new investigator. Although this can be expected and can be a source of esprit de corps as long as it's not allowed to get out of hand, having a formally trained investigator who actually *knows* how to perform the job can mean the difference between being able to take the ribbing and becoming disgruntled and not doing the job.

What Training Topics to Include

Training for the newly assigned investigator should emphasize those high-frequency tasks they will be expected to perform daily. These tasks include:

- **Report writing.** Keep in mind that new investigators are moving from a patrol-type report format to a pure narrative format. Information on the agency's investigative reporting and administrative paperwork system should also be included.
- **Interview and interrogation.** Patrol officers probably had some basic training in the police academy but may have never participated in a lengthy interview.
- **Surveillance techniques.** Rather than have them learn by doing or learn by messing up a surveillance, train them in the proper

techniques so that they make the majority of their initial mistakes during exercises, not an actual surveillance.

- **Use of official funds.** Due to the potential for problems in this area, it would be wise to include formal training in the agency's official fund policy and procedures.
- **Raid and arrest techniques.** This training should include not only the physical aspects of raids but also the planning aspects, such as operational plan development and safety considerations.
- **Confidential sources.** You cannot expect a new investigator to walk into a new assignment and successfully recruit, cultivate, and use confidential sources. Special emphasis should be placed on the agency's policy and procedures for using these critical sources of information.

Specific classes in various types of general assignment investigations would be beneficial as well. These classes could follow the generalized training. Training on specialty topics might pique the interest of new investigators to seek additional information on these topics. Specialty training topics relating to low-frequency activities could include sex crimes, narcotics, auto theft, identity theft, burglary, and the like.

PROBATIONARY PERIOD

When you consider that new patrol officers usually spend approximately 18 months to 2 years on probationary status, including a number of months under the tutelage of field training officers (FTOs), it makes sense that some type of a probationary period should also be applied to new investigators. Granted, there are major differences between a brand new patrol officer and a brand new investigator who is probably a veteran patrol officer with some years of experience, but a probationary period for a new investigator benefits both the officer and the agency. The benefit for the officer is that he or she gets an opportunity to see on a first-hand basis what investigators actually do daily. Sure, the new investigator has recently gone through a selection process in which he or she was made aware of the job description detailing what investigators do, but it is certainly not the same as actually doing it. Patrol officers often have a rather glamorous view of what investigators do, usually based on television, movies, and even on accounts of some investigators who choose to embellish their experiences to eager (and often impressionable) patrol officers. These glamorized views often contain daily search warrant executions, hostage situations, shootouts, and chases. Fortunately, reality is usually somewhat tamer, and the new investigator may need to learn that.

One of the best patrol officers I ever knew, a 20-year veteran who was still as aggressive as the day he hired on, was assigned to an investigative unit as a reward for his many years of outstanding service. I remember thinking how nice it was to see someone rewarded for great work, especially at this stage of his career. I happened to be working on a drug raid with his police department during one of his first few days as an investigator, and naturally he was assigned to come along. I remember how excited he was to be attending the preraid briefing and how carefully he listened and took notes on the written operational plan. During the raid, he performed professionally, as I knew that he would. Later that night over a few beers, he was still very excited, telling me that he should have gone into investigations years ago. It did my heart good to hear a 20-year veteran this excited. A few weeks later I stopped by the station. He was completing investigative reports. I asked how things were going, and he replied that he was "up to his eyeballs in paperwork" and that he couldn't believe how much paperwork there was to this "investigator business." About two months after that, I saw him again. I started to ask how things were going, but I didn't even get the question finished before he began complaining about the amount of paperwork, the fact that he hadn't arrested anybody in over a week, that he was bored stiff searching records for clues in a financial crimes case, and that, all things considered, he had been a lot better off in patrol.

Unfortunately, this department did not have a probationary period for investigators, which put both my friend and the investigative commander in a very sticky situation. If my friend asked to be reassigned to patrol, he'd lose face by looking like he was giving up because the assignment was too tough for him. If he was sent back to patrol by the commander, it would look like he was being returned because he couldn't hack it. Although neither of these reasons would be true, the *perceptions* would exist. Fortunately, he did go back to patrol, where he did his typical outstanding job, and he retired years later with his pride still intact after a great career as a patrol officer.

The probationary period also benefits the agency. You, the investigative manager, get an opportunity to see if the new investigator is suitable for the assignment. Particularly in agencies that use some type of a field training program, the skills and abilities of the new investigator can be objectively observed and evaluated. Although a comprehensive selection process screens for those skills and talents necessary for investigators and predictive of future success, no screening process is foolproof. Occasionally officers who aren't suitable squeak through the cracks. The probationary period can help evaluate these personnel and, if necessary, you can arrange for additional or remedial training or reassignment to a position for which they are better suited.

There is another element to keep in mind when considering a probationary period for new investigators. While the job of a patrol officer can sometimes be very solitary, particularly in agencies that have one-officer cars, the job of the investigator is seldom so. Investigators usually work in pairs or squads, and most of their time is spent working together. Investigators are sometimes under a great deal of stress, and the ability to interact with coworkers on a positive and professional basis when under stress is important. The probationary period is a good time to evaluate the ability of the new investigator to work with others and to get along with others.

TEMPORARY INVESTIGATIVE ASSIGNMENTS

Rarely have I seen an agency that has enough investigators to handle all of the cases assigned to the investigative unit. You can use some creative solutions to augment the investigative unit, such as temporary or rotational assignments, that have many long-term benefits to the individual officers as well as to the agency. Temporary assignments are where patrol officers are assigned to the investigative unit for periods ranging from 30 days to a year. This can be done on either a voluntary or rotational basis, so that as many patrol personnel as possible are given the opportunity to participate. For longer assignments, patrol officers receive some basic investigative training. For shorter assignments, the patrol officer simply might be assigned to work with an investigator with a directive to learn by watching and doing. I have used these programs with a great deal of success as a type of cross-training for patrol officers. The periods I have used have ranged from 30 days to 6 months.

There are many positive advantages to such a program. Temporary investigative assignments provide training for the participating patrol officer that is both in-house and economical. Another is that, after returning to patrol, patrol officers often conduct much better preliminary investigations. This is true because they have had the opportunity to see the other side and better realize how important thorough and professional preliminary investigations are to the follow-up efforts of the investigators. No amount of instruction will have as much of an impact as actually seeing the process firsthand. Another advantage is that a temporary investigative program can have a tremendous impact on the relations between the patrol and the investigative units. Communications are improved, both sides get a much better idea of what the other side does, and friendships are either formed or enhanced. All of these can lead to positive future benefits.

I recall one particularly cynical and negative patrol officer who took every opportunity to bad-mouth the investigators. He seemed to come up with as many derogatory comments as he could muster. If he wasn't complaining that they weren't doing anything, he was complaining about the fact they got a clothing allowance and all he ever saw them in was jeans and tee shirts. He used to joke about how many sets of golf clubs and/or picnic baskets they had in their unmarked squad cars. The time came for him to rotate into the investigative unit on a 90-day program. He was still complaining and poking fun at the investigators on the day he reported to his new assignment. That afternoon a road-rage incident ended when a 7-month-old infant was shot and critically wounded, and over the course of the next 3 months, whatever else could go wrong did go wrong. The investigators were incredibly busy with a variety of serious violent crimes and were working pretty much around the clock. By the end of the 90 days, this officer's attitude had changed considerably. At a potluck luncheon to bid him farewell on his return to patrol, he surprised everyone by standing up and admitting just how wrong he had been for all those years. He said his constant complaining about the investigators was not only rude and obnoxious, it was dead wrong. He went on to say that until he actually experienced it, he had no idea about the amount of work required to put together a prosecutable criminal case, particularly on a serious crime. He ended his remarks when he assured the investigators that the next time he heard one of his fellow patrol officers bad-mouthing investigators, he would immediately set them straight. What a ringing endorsement from a formerly critical individual!

A final advantage is that a temporary investigative program can increase morale. The prospect of driving around in a marked squad car for a 20- or 25-year career can be rather discouraging. Anything that offers new experiences and new challenges will usually be welcomed. The experience gained during a temporary assignment to investigations will no doubt benefit patrol officers when they return to patrol. The friendships they make will assist them throughout their careers. The "battery charge" that takes place by exposing them to another facet of police work can work wonders for a sometimes stale career. Finally, the temporary assignment to investigator can make the patrol officer feel more like part of the department, a feeling that is guaranteed to increase morale.

ROTATIONAL PROGRAMS

Many agencies rotate personnel out of task forces and into assignments with agencies such as the Drug Enforcement Administration, U.S. Customs, the FBI, and so on, but this rotational program is for positions *within the investigative unit.* An in-house rotational program means that a certain number of the positions in the investigator unit are set aside so that patrol officers can rotate into them for an extended period of time, usually 2–3 years. As an example, in an agency with six general assignment investigator positions, perhaps two or three are considering rotating positions, while the other three or four are considered non-rotating. (Notice that I did not use the term *permanent.* If you recall, the reasons for this were discussed in Chapter 3.)

A program such as this is a little more controversial, and some departments would be hard-pressed to implement it. A collective bargaining agreement may be in place that dictates which officers are assigned to investigative positions. This might seem that temporary or rotational positions are out of the question, but I feel these positions are important enough to discuss them with the union. In the agencies where I've seen temporary or rotational positions implemented, these positions have worked out well, with the positive aspects far outweighing the negative. New blood in the investigative unit can:

• Bring an enhanced spirit and a new work ethic to the unit
• Cause less-than-stellar investigators to begin working again, lest they be "run over" by the zealous new workers
• Resurrect older, unsolved cases by having them reviewed and perhaps reworked by newer personnel.

For a rotational program such as this, I would recommend some type of screening or selection process be used, perhaps similar to the investigator selection process outlined in Chapter 4. This ensures the most talented personnel are selected.

When a patrol officer is rotated into an investigator position, they should receive basic investigative training to equip them with the knowledge to perform the basic tasks. Specialty training, such as narcotics, auto theft, and the like, is something that you could consider later. Since this is an extended assignment, it is important that the patrol officer is treated like an investigator, complete with identification, manner of dress, vehicle, and all other tools of the job.

There are some potential problems with this program. The first and most obvious is the impact on those investigators whose current positions will be subject to the rotation. If existing investigators are displaced to make room for patrol officers, it will generate some hard feelings. In some cases, particularly if the investigator being rotated out will lose salary or other benefits, you might anticipate a legal challenge. In the event that the position of investigator is a permanent rank, you can expect a legal challenge. You can, however, establish a rotational program even in these situations. You can start by establishing one position assigned to a patrol officer rotating into the unit. You then create other rotating positions as other investigators retire, are promoted, or otherwise move on to other opportunities. By doing this, you ultimately achieve a balance of nonrotating and rotating personnel to whatever ratio you feel is appropriate. It may take a few years to accomplish this goal, but the long-term benefits to the agency are usually worth the effort.

Before establishing a rotational program for some of the investigator positions in an investigative unit, however, there are certain questions you must answer:

1. How many investigators to rotate? This is difficult to estimate. You must consider the types of crime encountered, frequency of crime that is referred for follow-up investigation, and workload of the investigators. Some agencies rotate all of their investigator positions on a 3- to 5-year basis. The problem with this approach is that you may never really have a strong cadre of experienced investigators available. Other agencies rotate only a few positions, thereby limiting the rotational program under the guise of maintaining a strong group of experienced investigators. You need to balance the needs of the unit with the goal of the rotational program, which is to offer more opportunities to deserving patrol officers. For an agency with six investigators working general assignment duties, two or three rotational positions might make sense.

2. **How long should the rotation be?** This is another difficult consideration. The problem with a too-short rotation of perhaps a year is that by the time the new investigator learns enough to actually sink his teeth into investigations, it's time to rotate back to patrol. A 2-year rotation is better, but even that may lead to productivity issues. Based on my observations, it takes about 6 months for a patrol officer to get comfortable enough to work cases independently. The next year is spent working in earnest, and the final 6 months is spent cleaning up their work in preparation for rotating back to patrol. In the final analysis, you only get about a year's worth of investigative work out of the officer.

   In my opinion, a 3-year rotation is ideal. When I was assigned as the director of a very large metropolitan narcotics task force, we rotated patrol officers from suburban police departments every 2 years. One of my first official acts as task force director was to seek approval to extend the rotation period to 3 years. The request was approved, and the productivity of the task force increased a great deal. A 3-year rotation doesn't severely limit the number of personnel able to take advantage of the program, and it allows for approximately 2 solid years of working as an investigator. I feel the 3-year period gives participating officers enough time to develop experience and skills that they will carry through the remainder of his or her career.

3. **What about the loss of experience?** This should not be a problem if you've reasonably estimated the number of positions to be rotated. In fact, the balance of the experience of the older investigators and the exuberance and excitement of the newly rotated

patrol officers often improve the unit's overall productivity. If you have several rotating positions, one possible solution is to stagger the assignments. One officer could start a rotation this year, another officer could start in the subsequent year, and so on. This allows for some continuity within the unit and wouldn't saddle you with too many new personnel at one time.

4. **What happens when investigators rotate out?** As already mentioned, this can cause bad blood. In some cases, the hurt feelings might run deep enough that the officer leaving the unit decides to "lay down" on their return to patrol duties. In these cases, monitoring and documenting their performance deficiencies might (unfortunately) be the only course of action available.

Positions in any law enforcement agency should never be viewed as permanent by anyone. Occasionally, personnel are given assignments they neither want nor like. As unfortunate as this may be, law enforcement, being a paramilitary-type organization, cannot be run strictly by assigning people only to those positions in which they will be happy. It just can't work that way. It has been my experience that personnel who carry a grudge are the minority. In most cases, the opposite holds true. Officers moved to patrol to make room for rotating positions hit the ground running and perform admirably. Granted, they might not be the happiest workers in the department, but their personal pride, dedication to the profession, and a strong desire not to let down their fellow cops motivates them to perform well.

From a personnel assessment standpoint, losing a permanent investigator in order to establish a rotating position might have a hidden benefit. The officer who returns to the patrol assignment with a good attitude and a solid work ethic is a valuable employee and you should recognize that person as such. I have always believed that the true measure of one's character is not how well they perform a task that they *enjoy* performing, but rather how well they perform a task that they *don't enjoy.*

I have observed situations in which investigators being returned to patrol assignments have "hit the ground running" and used all of the skills that they acquired in the investigative assignment on their patrol assignments. Unfortunately I have also observed situations in which the investigator being returned has done so with an extremely poor attitude and has moped and whined about their perceived misfortune for quite a while. Most people do eventually get out of this stage, however some never do.

5. **What happens if they can't cut it?** The rotating investigator position should be subject to the same probationary status as any other position. These positions should also include training by a few (several if possible) Field Training Officers, who are themselves investigators. After all, this is a 3-year assignment; the additional training and observation can be beneficial. By combining the probationary period and the FTO evaluations, it will become readily apparent if a new rotating investigator is unsuitable. If this occurs, he or she can easily be removed from the rotation and the next officer on the list can be given his or her opportunity.

I can remember one patrol officer who had all of the tools to succeed as an investigator. He was extremely "streetwise," wrote excellent reports, was very intelligent, and had the ability to handle people from nearly every walk of life. His downfall, however, was his rather active social life, and as soon as he was assigned to the rotating tactical position he began to quiz his supervisors on how many weekend nights he would be able to take off during the summer. This was even after the assignment was thoroughly explained to him, including the part about tactical officers working most, if not all, weekends. Apparently he had either been engaging in "selective hearing," or didn't take the job description given to him seriously. In any event, he lasted about three months of the three-year assignment, and was sent back to his patrol assignment.

As has been pointed out, I've always believed that the most difficult thing for managers of a small to mid sized police department to do is to keep the job interesting. The inclusion of a rotational program, whether it be long or short-term, can go a long way in demonstrating to personnel that there is in fact an opportunity for them to do something different in their careers. In some cases this will result in personnel being able to demonstrate their potential for becoming an excellent investigator. In other cases it will result in people demonstrating that are probably not very well suited for consideration for investigative assignments.

Regardless, if either of these things occur, the opportunity to participate in a rotational assignment to investigations will provide good exposure to investigations to patrol personnel. This will provide them a much better basis for them to make up their mind whether to pursue an investigative position when the opportunity arises.

Chapter 8

SUPERVISING INVESTIGATIVE PERSONNEL

The principles of managing investigative personnel may be the same, the supervisory techniques might be the same, and the position of formal authority in the agency might be the same, but little of this matters to new supervisors or managers who fail to realize that when it comes to managing investigative units, a different management style is definitely needed.

Having the privilege to teach classes for a variety of law enforcement managers all over the world provides me with the opportunity to "do some research" by seeing how the participants in the various classes feel about a variety of topics. When I talk about "Supervision of Investigative Personnel," I always begin the discussion with a quote:

True or False: "Supervision of Investigative Personnel is not only different, it is usually more difficult than supervision of patrol Personnel." The responses that I get are very interesting, as they run the gamut from total agreement with the statement to total disagreement.

Most investigative managers have also, at some point in their careers, also supervised patrol personnel. This affords them the opportunity to see the differences inherent in both types of supervision and management. Many feel that supervision of patrol personnel is much more difficult, for several reasons:

- Patrol is where the newer personnel are assigned, which means closer supervision, more time spent on observation and correcting performance.

- Patrol is often very fast-paced, and surprises during the shift are the rule as opposed to being the exception.
- Patrol is a function that results in many more contacts with citizens, in a variety of circumstances, which means more chances for negative interactions that result in complaints against police personnel.
- Investigators, as a rule, have more experience, more time on the job, and are less likely to need "hands-on" supervision and observation.
- The fact that we target the "best and brightest" in our selection strategies for investigators makes them easier to supervise.

Some investigative managers, however, feel that the greater level of experience and background that is possessed by most investigative personnel leads to a much more difficult time supervising or managing them, due to their (sometimes) self-perceived "prima donna" status. This sometimes exhibits itself in their resistance to even the most even-handed and cursory supervision.

The fact is that the supervision or management of investigative personnel need not be any more difficult, as long as it is recognized and acknowledged to be "different" than supervision or management of patrol personnel. Not easier, not harder, just "different."

A DIFFERENT MANAGEMENT STYLE

Whenever I come across a student recently assigned to an investigative management position with little or no investigative background, I always ask them who they must have irritated to have deserved such a fate, and I'm only half-joking. The difficulty is that to successfully manage investigators, you must know what makes them tick. As was mentioned in the preface, it often seems that the real difference between patrol officers and investigators oftentimes comes down to this: Patrol officers merely *think* that they know everything. Investigators, on the other hand, are *absolutely certain* they know everything, and equally as certain that patrol officers know nothing. Although this is a somewhat humorous way of looking at the differences, if you cut through the sarcasm there is a kernel of truth in the statement. It is only when new supervisors or managers come to grips with this fact that they will begin to understand the investigator's psyche.

Supervisors or managers that come from a patrol background are used to a situation in which they are supervising a set number of personnel, who are assigned to set areas, for a set amount of time. For the most part, when that set time is finished, these personnel go home. Patrol officers are closely supervised and must document their whereabouts at all times. When officers are out of their vehicles for any reason, including meals and bathroom breaks, they must notify communications where they are and what they're doing. From a supervisory standpoint, this is an orderly and uncomplicated system.

The problems begin when the newly assigned investigative manager attempts to instill this fixed and orderly style of supervision on the investigative unit. Investigators, by necessity, need a great deal more autonomy. They don't operate in such a structured environment. Investigative leads can take them almost anywhere at a moment's notice.

This looser structure is enhanced by the fact that the selection process for investigators usually targets the self-thinkers and brightest of the patrol force. These personnel usually don't operate well in a very strict and fixed environment. Too much supervision can often stifle the imagination, initiative, and efforts of many investigators. You shouldn't adopt a completely hands-off method of supervision, however, because investigators still must be accountable. Such controls should not be so stifling as to negatively impact the need for autonomy and freedom required by any investigative assignment.

MAKING INVESTIGATORS ACCOUNTABLE

Investigators must be trustworthy enough to work with minimum supervision. Regardless of the need for freedom, you need to make investigators accountable for their actions and movements. Although tracking the whereabouts and activities of investigators is inherently more challenging than for patrol officers, tracking investigators' time doesn't have to be difficult. Why is accountability for the activities of investigators so important? There are several reasons:

- **Proper accountability decreases "slide time."** There isn't an investigator anywhere who doesn't take some advantage of the fact that they have more freedom of movement than their brother and sister officers in patrol assignments. Whether this means stopping by the store for something while on duty, getting their hair cut, picking up cleaning, and the like, the fact that they don't have to account for their whereabouts every minute of their duty day as they did in patrol will lead to some small abuses of their time. Most investigative supervisors and managers don't have a problem with this, as long as it remains reasonable. The problem starts if and when there are no control mechanisms and the investigators begin to feel that they have nobody at all keeping track of what they're doing.
- **Proper accountability makes performance evaluations easier.** Most performance evaluation instruments include a time management component. I believe this is one of the most important attributes for an investigator. Investigators who cannot properly manage their own time no doubt will fall behind on their workloads, will not address their cases professionally, and have a host of other problems. Maintaining accountability over the time and activities of investigators should be minimal, but it also should be considered when evaluating their overall performance.
- **Proper accountability can be an excellent management tool.** Accountability controls can be utilized for management studies, crime analysis, planning, and budgeting, and they can provide solid evidence when you request things like equipment, training, and/or additional personnel. Gone are the days when any manager can simply ask for something and expect to get it. Tighter budgets and the philosophy of do more with less means that managers must justify their requests. Proper accountability over the activities of investigative personnel will provide you with the data necessary for these justifications.

Any control mechanisms for investigators must be both *mandatory* and *simple*. It can be as simple as fill-in-the-blank activity reports or something as sophisticated as a computerized timekeeping system. Whatever the format, all you'll need is some mechanism to track case numbers, crime codes, activity codes, times, dates, and the identity of the investigator.

The timeliness of these activity reports can also be critical. Some agencies have their investigative personnel fill out a daily activity log that details what they've done each day. Other agencies feel that this is too time-consuming and utilize a weekly format instead. Others use a monthly activity report. There are problems associated with each type. Some investigative personnel would no doubt feel that a daily report is excessive when taking into account the level of freedom and autonomy that they enjoy as part of their daily duties. With a monthly format, there's too much chance that the investigators will wait until the last few days of the month to fill them out and then try to reconstruct their activity for an entire month in a half hour's time. That is exactly what I did when I worked under such a system. On one of the last days of the month, my partner and I would sit there and try our best to remember what we were doing three weeks ago last Thursday. It actually became quite comical and led to some very creative record-keeping, at the obvious expense of accuracy.

Perhaps a weekly format might be best for most agencies. Keep in mind, however, that if you plan to use the Manpower Allocation Method for determining appropriate staffing levels (as discussed in Chapter 3), timekeeping must be accurate or the formula will not work. Similar to fire drills, the goal of any accountability mechanism is to get people to do them without thinking about them. Whatever mechanism you decide to use will be more accurate if it is kept simple and if it ultimately becomes a part of the routine of the investigator.

SPAN OF CONTROL

Anyone who has ever taken Police Supervision 101 has learned the old standby formula that the typical span of control over subordinates is 8-10 police officers for one supervisor. This might be suitable for patrol personnel, but it is often excessive for investigators. I subscribe to the statement that *there is an inverse correlation between span of control and the complexity of the work being accomplished.* In other words, the span of control over personnel performing less complex functions can be larger. I'm not saying that the work of patrol officers is easier then the work of investigators, but I am saying it is generally not as complex. When you take into account the complexities of the work being done and some of the investigations being conducted, a ratio of 5–7 investigators might be more realistic. A smaller span of control can (and should) lead to better supervision, better accountability for the activities of subordinates, and a more accurate review of accomplishments.

Consider some other elements when determining your span of control. One is the number of specialty assignments. Although the supervisor or manager is not expected to be an expert in each of the specialties to which their personnel may be assigned, it is reasonable to suggest that the supervisor should have a working knowledge in each of the specialties. The more specialties, the more knowledge the supervisor must possess. An excessive number of specialties can make for an excessive work load for even the best and most talented supervisor or manager. Another element to consider is the physical locations of investigators. If you are responsible for personnel in several different locations, the number of personnel you can effectively manage is diminished due to the travel time between these locations. This time is not spent working or supervising; it is wasted traveling.

For example, I was once responsible for four squads of investigators. With a direct report span of control of only four squad supervisors, this shouldn't have been very difficult. The problem was that this particular assignment covered both of the problems just mentioned: too many specialties and too many locations. The squads specialized in auto theft, child sex crimes, fugitive apprehension, and one general assignment squad. To compound matters, one squad was located in the center of Chicago, another on the north side, another in the far southern suburbs, and the remaining squad in the western suburbs. I spent more time driving from one location to another than I did supervising or managing, and I know that the level of management I was able to provide suffered as a result. It was one of the worst assignments I ever had. Not because of the personnel, who were all professional, talented, and extremely successful, but because I tried to be everywhere at once. It didn't work.

Chapter 9

CASE MANAGEMENT

I remember sitting in a pub with a few cop friends one evening, having dinner after a search warrant execution. One of them remarked, "Man, what a way to make a living . . . buy yourself a pub, hire some people to run it for you, and sit back, drink free beer and watch the money roll in." Obviously this guy had no concept whatsoever of what it takes to run a business: long hours, employee problems, insurance issues, profit margins, and so on. Unfortunately, the same approach is sometimes taken to case management, when some investigative managers take the approach, "Man, what a great assignment. All I do is assign these cases and watch the arrests and convictions roll in."

Case management refers to actually *managing* all of the investigations the unit is assigned. The duties associated with this management include:

- Case screening
- Case assignment
- Investigative managers carry caseloads
- Case reporting
- Using an investigative filing system
- Securing investigative information
- Investigative planning
- Case review
- Case status.

To manage an investigative unit, all of these tasks must be done correctly and simultaneously. This can be nerve-racking and difficult, but then nobody said that managing an investigative unit was easy. By keeping in mind that the investigative process is really no more than the sum of all these parts, if you address the individual parts correctly, the overall process should run relatively smoothly.

CASE SCREENING

Perhaps the first (and many would say the most important) element of the investigative process is case screening. The investigators as-3signed to the unit are without question the most valuable resource and should be utilized as efficiently and effectively as possible. A policy covering investigative responsibilities governs what matters are referred to the investigative unit by patrol. Case screening, however, examines which cases should be assigned for follow-up investigations. In other words, case screening determines the workload of the entire investigative unit.

The screening process need not be elaborate. It can be a simple form you or your designee fill out following a review of the initial incident report normally completed by a patrol officer. The following form, developed by a detective manager at an agency where I was chief of police, is simple. It's a mechanism to assign point values to information regarding the incident to determine if you should assign an investigator to the case. (See the example provided in Appendix 6.) As part of the screening process, and particularly for cases that do not meet the criteria for assignment for follow-up investigation, you should make some contact with the crime victim. Victims of crimes, no matter how minor, often feel violated. Some type of contact from the police over and above the initial contact by the patrol officer can go a long way toward enhancing or improving the relationship between citizens and the police department.

The purpose of the follow-up contact is to advise the victim either that the matter has been assigned for follow-up investigation and to identify the investigator or to advise the crime victim that the matter has been reviewed and it does not appear that enough leads exist to warrant a follow-up investigation by an investigator. It also gives the crime victim a chance to give any additional information that may provide further leads or to report the discovery of additional missing property. This contact can be done either by phone or in writing, and it need not be done by an investigator. In fact, it can easily be formatted into a template and saved in the computer. When a letter needs to be generated, it can be personalized, printed, and sent by a member of the clerical staff. (See the examples provided in Appendix 7 and Appendix 8.)

The important thing is that the follow-up contact does occur, as this is what the public has every right to expect. If there is no follow-up, who could blame the citizen/victim if they felt that they were nothing but a "number" and that the agency did not care about them or their problems?

The citizen doesn't care who wrote the correspondence, who sent it, or quite frankly, what's in it–they just want to feel that *someone* is taking the time to pay some attention to them. The good feelings that are generated by taking the time to correspond with crime victims don't just apply to the victim themselves. Just like any other contact with the police, the feelings that the victim will have from receiving some type of follow-up contact will be shared with their family, neighbors, or almost anyone with whom they come into contact.

CASE ASSIGNMENT

Case assignment is much easier if all the investigators are specialists, set up primarily to handle one type of investigation. This is rare except in very large investigative units. In most small to mid-sized investigative units, investigators are generalists; they investigate a wide variety of offenses. If you manage this type of unit, you must carefully assign your cases, because a number of negative consequences can result from improper assignments. If you have generalist investigators, you should take into account the following information when assigning cases:

- **Aptitude of the investigator.** You must see that the cases are investigated thoroughly and professionally. To identify and assign the most capable investigator, you should consider the aptitudes of the people in your unit. For example, in supervising narcotics investigators for a number of years, I noted that there seemed to be two categories of narcotics investigators: what I call the hit-and-run narcs and the long-term narcs. The hit-and-run narcotics investigators would make a buy then make an arrest, or make a buy then hit the place with a search warrant. They would move from case to case in this manner, always active, always looking for the next arrest. They didn't handle inactivity or office time well at all. They instead wanted to be out on the street, locking up the bad guys.

The "long-term" narcotics investigators, on the other hand, could work for months or even years making a conspiracy case on an offender or a group of offenders. They would spend countless hours reviewing records, conducting surveillance or overhears of telephone conversations, and whatever else needed to be done. They held off their arrests until the culmination of the investigation. Rarely did I come across a narcotics investigator who enjoyed doing both. Instead they fell into one category or the other, so the aptitude of the investigator must be considered when assigning cases so that you assign the most capable person.

- **Complexity of the investigation.** Some investigations are much more difficult to complete than others. You must assign the most complex cases to the investigators capable of the careful analysis and critical thinking that must be applied to these cases.

  Consider again the example of the narcotics investigators. Although I don't want to diminish the types of investigations conducted by the hit-and-run narcs, I do believe that the long-term conspiracy cases were more complex. By the same token, a very involved check or credit card fraud case or an identity theft case might be so complex that it requires someone with the mentality of the long-term narc. By properly assessing the ability of the investigator and applying it to the complexity of the case, you're increasing your chances that the case will be properly assigned, which in turn increases the chances that it will be investigated successfully.

- **Special interests of the investigator.** If given the opportunity, you might take into account the special interests of your investigators when determining case assignment. If an investigator has a certain interest and has developed skills in working with computers, you might assign crimes involving computers to him or her. An investigator who is a car buff might receive cases involving auto theft. However, you must use caution when using special interests as a factor. The potential negative is that the investigator might get so involved in their special interest or hobby that they lose sight of the fact that they're investigating a crime. They're having fun with their special interest or hobby, and occasionally they might need a reality check to make certain that they haven't lost sight of their original goal, which is to solve the crime.

One aspect of case management that you must guard against is *inequitable caseloads.* As a manager, there is nothing worse than coming to the realization that the work in the investigative unit has been inequitably assigned, especially since this is often brought to your attention by disgruntled investigators. This can have a devastating impact on morale. Seldom will investigators who feel that they're being treated unfairly keep it to themselves. Instead they become very vocal expressing that they are being treated unfairly. They will complain, "How can Investigator so-and-so sit at his desk while I'm working my butt off?"

You must also be careful in how you assign what I call heater cases. A heater case is one that is going to generate a great deal of interest (heat) from the media, the public, politicians, or the hierarchy of the police department. If the same investigator gets all of these assignments, it can have a detrimental impact on the morale of the rest of the unit. In addition, you must consider how this is being perceived by the investigator to whom all of the heaters are being assigned. They may initially feel very flattered that they're being given the most high profile and complex cases, but only to the point where they start feeling the work is unfairly assigned. They can then develop the perception that you're taking unfair advantage of their talent and skills.

I have a personal situation that illustrates this point. I was assigned to command a unit that had several very talented investigators. In one of the squads was an outstanding investigator who could handle anything that was assigned to him. "Tommy" was a veteran police officer who had spent a large portion of his career in investigative assignments. He could successfully interact with people from any station in life, and could interview suspects as successfully as anyone I'd ever seen. He was able to write timely, thorough, and excellent reports, and he was capable of working undercover very well. He was a joy to supervise, because he needed little if any supervision. In short, "Tommy" had it all. So I began to assign all of the heater cases to him, and he responded beautifully. He always exceeded expectations and did an outstanding job. The victims were happy, the upper command was happy, the media was happy, and I was happy.

You can imagine my chagrin on the day that he presented me with a request for transfer to a patrol assignment. I was crushed! Not only was "Tommy" a great investigator, but over the years we had become close friends. I was personally hurt that he'd want to leave the unit. I was even more hurt when I realized that I had caused it. When I asked why he wanted the transfer, he told me that he was burned out and that he was tired of having all the heater cases. He indicated that at first he was flattered that I had so much confidence in his abilities but that it began to get old very quickly when he realized that all of the most difficult investigations ended up in his caseload. The end result was that I recommended that his transfer be approved and he left the unit, finishing his career in a patrol assignment. Fortunately for me, the error I had made by inequitably assigning cases didn't cost me the friendship, but I learned a very valuable lesson about case assignment.

One method of seeing to it that the less experienced investigators gain exposure to heater cases is to make team assignments. In other words, the case is assigned to a less experienced investigator and an experienced veteran. The less experienced investigator is given the overall responsibility for the case but benefits from the knowledge, expertise, and counseling of the more experienced veteran. Regarding the equitable distribution of the general caseload, you can use the case review process to balance the work. This process will be discussed shortly.

Another method is to assign cases on a rotational basis. While this doesn't relieve you from considering who the most capable person is to handle a case, it does help avoid overloading some investigators while leaving others with too little work. There are some inherent problems with a strict rotational policy for case assignment, however, and these should not be overlooked. Sometimes with a policy of strict rotational assignment, an investigator can be assigned to an investigation that they don't really possess the skill or ability to be able to handle. I learned this lesson the hard way, and it could have been disastrous.

I happened to be speaking with an investigator and his unit manager and the investigator brought up an ongoing investigation, telling me that I'd probably be getting a call from a relative of the victim. When I asked for further details I was told that it was a possible sexual assault and the family of the victim wasn't happy with the progress of the investigation. As the unit manager was leaving I pulled him aside and asked if he minded if I discussed the case with the investigator and possibly offered some suggestions. He told me that not only would he not mind, he'd appreciate it, as he knew that I had a background which included commanding a unit that investigated child sexual exploitation.

As I spoke to the investigator assigned to the case, it became very apparent that he had overlooked numerous potential leads, not due to any lack of talent on his part, as he was an extremely intelligent investigator, but more due to lack of experience with this type of investigation.

Following our conversation, in which I made some suggestions for the investigation, I suggested that we conduct an "investigative conference" with the immediate family to answer their questions and to assure them that we were in fact working the investigation thoroughly. The investigator and the investigative manager reluctantly agreed, and we set a time for the conference.

During the investigative conference, we outlined to the family what had been done thus far on the investigation as well as our plans for future activity. When that was completed, I asked if they had any questions or suggestions for us. One of the relatives looked at the investigator assigned and asked if he had interviewed the possible witness whose name they had provided two weeks prior. The investigator simply said "No" and when asked why he hadn't been in contact with this potential witness he stated that he had no reason, he just hadn't done it. This was followed by a few more questions from another family member regarding information that they had provided and they received the same response–the information had not been persued.

Needless to say, myself and the unit manager were extremely embarrassed, and quite unhappy with this unexpected turn of events. After the family left, the unit manager and I sat down and he began to apologize. I simply asked how this investigator had been assigned this particular case, considering his lack of background and training to conduct such an investigation. The answer I received was "it was his turn on the rotation for case assignment" which quite frankly didn't make me any happier. I told the unit manager that it was therefore our fault that this case had not been handled properly. It was our fault because we should have known better than to assign an extremely complex and high profile investigation such as this to someone who didn't have the background to properly investigate it. This was an extremely valuable, albeit painful, lesson learned regarding case assignment.

Perhaps the biggest problem with inequitable caseloads is that sooner or later you will be in the unenviable position of having to transfer cases. Transferring cases from one investigator to another has the potential for disaster. First of all, it's embarrassing for you if you have to reassign cases because they were improperly assigned. The person from whom you're taking the case may think you believe they "can't hack it," that you have to reassign their work to someone else so it gets done. If they feel the other investigators in the unit share this perception, it can be very demoralizing. The investigator to whom you transfer the case may perceive they are being "dumped on," having to finish what someone else has started when they've got their own work to do. They also may have sympathy for the investigator who originally had the case, feeling that that person has been disrespected. In both scenarios, you will be the one who ultimately feels the brunt of their collective disapproval. The only way that cases can be successfully transferred is to first insist that all work is properly documented, which leads to the next aspect of case management: case reporting.

INVESTIGATIVE MANAGERS CARRYING CASELOADS

In many agencies, due to lack of manpower or other resources, investigative managers must carry their own caseloads, in addition to their managerial duties. This is very common in smaller agencies or in many specialized units, and although in these cases the agency might not have a choice but to do this, there are some disadvantages which should not be overlooked.

Less time to actually observe the work of subordinates. One of the primary functions of any manager is to observe the work of subordinates. Without this observation, performance evaluations cannot be completed fairly, training needs will not be identified, and shortcomings will not be addressed.

Possibility of getting bogged down in a lengthy investigation. This will further remove the opportunity for the investigative manager to actually *manage* the investigative unit. This can lead to poor decisions by investigative managers, inappropriate allocation of personnel and other resources, and a breakdown in the overall management of the unit. The investigative manager gets so involved in the long-term investigation that they don't have time for anything else, which is particularly true if the long-term investigation is very high-profile or complex.

Can negatively impact case review and other elements of case management. Many of the elements of case management, such as case review, aren't exactly the "fun part" of managing an investigative unit. They are, however, critical to the unit's success and must be accomplished. Investigative managers who are carrying their own caseloads often have the time that they should be devoting to case management taken away by their caseload, which creates a great deal of difficulty.

Can interfere with necessary interaction with upper management. Part of the responsibility of investigative managers is to interact as needed with upper management. This interaction is for the purposes of keeping upper management appraised of the unit's activities, discussing the need for additional resources or training, and a host of other issues. When the investigative manager's caseload precludes them from conducting this interaction, the entire investigative unit can suffer.

In the event that it becomes necessary for the investigative manager to carry a caseload, whether it be due to manpower, size of agency, workload, or other concerns, careful selection of the cases assigned to the investigative manager should be considered. This will not alleviate or remove some of these concerns, but could prevent problems in the future.

CASE REPORTING

In most instances, the standard reporting format used by patrol officers (fill-in-the-blank and a short narrative report) is not adequate for investigators. Given the nature of investigative reports, there is a greater need for a narrative format. Most investigative reporting formats almost entirely consist of narrative, which can be intimidating for the new investigator. If not intimidating, these reports will most likely be unfamiliar to the new member of the unit. One solution is to prepare a case reporting manual. This need not be elaborate. It can simply be a three-ring binder that contains all forms used by the unit, instructions for their proper completion, and samples of completed forms. Besides being a valuable training aid, this manual can aid in consistency and standardization of reporting which will make reviews easier.

There are basically two types of investigative reports. First is a compilation of effort, where the entire investigation is completed and one report is written to reflect all activity accomplished. The second type is individualized reporting of each event. This is a separate report for each action taken, such as a report for each interview, surveillance, search warrant execution, and so on. There are advantages and disadvantages to each type of reports. These are shown in the following tables.

Table 9.1
COMPILATION-OF-EFFORT REPORT

Advantages	Disadvantages
The report consists of one single document completed at the conclusion of the investigation.	There is a tendency to procrastinate and therefore forget details, as the reports might be completed days or even weeks after the activity.
There is less bulk, although there may be more attachments.	Incompleteness of reports may result, in that some small details might be omitted.
Some people think it's easier to sit and write the entire report at one time, as opposed to switching from investigative mode to report-writing mode frequently.	There may be a tendency to synopsize rather than report, omitting small details for the sake of brevity.

Table 9.2
INDIVIDUALIZED REPORTING OF EACH EVENT

Advantages	*Disadvantages*
Generally, the reports are more detailed because the report is being completed immediately after the activity.	This style involves much more writing. The completed case reports are bulkier because more reports are being completed.
Timeliness usually means better recollection of the details.	Some people consider this a harder way to write reports, as opposed to waiting for the entire investigation to be completed and then writing one comprehensive report.
There is a much better chance that all details will be included in the report.	This style is definitely more time-consuming, in that there is a "break in the investigative action" at the conclusion of the activity to take time to complete the report.

Regardless of which style you use, an investigative summary document of some type needs to be completed when the case is closed or referred for prosecution or to another agency. This investigative summary need not be elaborate. It should simply be a document that gives the reader a quick view of the facts. Items such as the following should be included:

• Summary of the investigation
• Listing of evidentiary items including the chain of custody
• Defendant's criminal history
• List of witnesses
• Table of contents of reports and documents.

Typically, this investigative summary is placed on top of the individual reports and other case documents, which are numbered and listed on the table of contents of the summary. The prosecutor or agency to which the case is referred is therefore provided with a package of the entire investigation.

There are a few advantages to generating an investigative summary:

• **By providing a set format for reporting, the investigative summary ensures completeness and attention to detail.** Investigators will not be able to forget certain elements, which is common in lengthy reports. The required sections are clearly spelled out for the report writer.

- **The finished package is organized and clear.** This makes it much easier for prosecutors/referred agencies to get an immediate grasp of the facts. Rather than wading through a pile of papers, whoever receives this package will be able to quickly select the reports that need immediate review. They simply view the table of contents and select the pertinent information. When a prosecutor is conducting a preliminary hearing, they usually don't need to digest the entire document, just the most crucial individual reports. This investigative summary allows them to do just that.

These investigative summaries are not only useful for criminal investigations, but they can also be used for noncriminal matters such as background investigation, liquor/business license investigations, and the like. As a former police and fire commissioner, I can tell you that when background investigations on police and fire applicants were presented along with an investigative summary, the review and selection process was a lot more organized and went much smoother. The only disadvantage I can think of is that an investigative summary requires a little more work, but it is definitely worth the effort. (See the example provided in Appendix 9.)

There are a few reporting issues to consider. First, it seems common for most police departments to have a resident computer expert who often takes it upon him or herself to generate his or her own unofficial forms. This should be avoided because it leads to confusion. If you decide to use these unofficial forms, make sure that all involved personnel "staff" and review the documents prior to using them. By "staffing" the document, I mean the document should be reviewed by command officers of the unit. I would also recommend having some members of the investigative unit review and edit the forms. This should be done to make certain that these unofficial forms are actually necessary and suit the purposes for which they were designed. If these reviews do not take place, these new forms might be missing critical elements.

Second, be careful how you handle investigative notes. These are the rough notes taken during an investigation that are ultimately reduced to a finished final report. They may be notes taken during an interview, during surveillance, or at any other time. It has always been my position that—barring the wishes of prosecutors, department policy, or statutes to the contrary—these notes should be destroyed once the final reports are completed. The reason for the destruction is that these notes may be discoverable in a court case. Minor discrepancies between the notes and final report might not have any real bearing on the investigation, but once these discrepancies are in the hands of a skillful defense attorney, they can wreak havoc on your prosecution. As long as this is *always* done, or is a part of written policy, the practice usually presents no problems in court.

USING AN INVESTIGATIVE FILING SYSTEM

I have seen time and time again that reliance on the standard agency filing system is not always advisable. Question regarding security of information, access by unauthorized personnel, and "need to know" of persons handling investigative reports sometimes arise if the investigative case files are merely part of the overall PD filing system. It is usually better for investigations units to have a separate filing system for their ongoing/open/pending investigations. In order to be effective, the investigative filing system must be:

- **Complete.** All investigative documentation, from the case opening document to the final report, must be included. There can be no other filing system for investigative reports; they must be maintained in the same system.
- **Easy to understand.** If the investigative filing system is too complex, people won't use it properly, and the security of the information becomes a potential disaster.
- **Secure from compromise.** The files must be safe from access, view, and alteration by unauthorized personnel.

Besides active/closed/archival case files, the following files should be considered for the investigative division:

1. **Administrative files.** The information contained in applications for business licenses and liquor licenses can be very useful for investigators. Unfortunately, however, these records are usually kept at the city clerk's office and are not accessible during non-business hours. Maintaining copies of these documents in the investigative unit's filing system or computer database can pro-

vide the desired information at any time of the day or night. These records will naturally have to be kept up to date, but this administrative task need not be done by an investigator.

2. **Warrant files.** I'm not speaking of active arrest warrants, which will be maintained in some type of computer database, but rather copies of past affidavits for search warrants, requests for overhear orders, and so on. These documents, particularly if maintained electronically, can be very useful as templates for similar situations in the future. If you think about it, there are only so many different circumstances in which one of these items (search warrant, overhear order, etc.) will be needed, and the basis for the request (probable cause) won't change that much. Why reinvent the wheel every time such a document is needed? Having these templates available will save investigators a great deal of time.

3. **Confidential source files.** These must be kept secure and separate, with limited, controlled, and necessary access.

4. **Modus operandi (M.O.) files.** These are very useful when investigating similar crimes. They need not be elaborate, but should contain information regarding the specific modus operandi of selected crimes. For example, if an identified burglar uses channel-lock-type pliers to circumvent apartment doors in a multifamily dwelling, it would be advisable to include this fact in some sort of database. In the event a similar crime is discovered in the future, at least the investigator assigned will have someplace to start. While M.O. files might not be practical for very large agencies, they would probably be very beneficial for small to midsized agencies.

One more type of file needs to be mentioned here. These are *street files,* separate case files maintained personally by the investigator conducting the investigation. They often consist of rough notes or other documents. These should be discouraged if not forbidden, as their very existence can sometimes have a disastrous impact on investigations, prosecution, and even on the police department. The basic problem is that these street files often don't contain *exactly* the same information that is in the official case file. These differences are usually completely innocent and/or inadvertent, but defense attorneys love to see these minor discrepancies. Seldom are these street files submitted in response to a request for discovery, and therein lies the problem. If the existence of these street files becomes known, as it often has, the minor discrepancies suddenly become huge issues that can seriously hamper the prosecution of the case.

You must insist that *all* case documents be included in the case file. If this is not monitored closely, documents relating to the case may be lost. In addition, if the case is transferred to another investigator and all of the documents are not in the file, the investigator's job becomes much more difficult. Keep in mind that *believing* that the work is being done is not the same as *actually seeing* the finished product in the case file.

In addition to seeing to it that all case documents are properly filed, you must control and document access to and copying from files. Use of some type of check-out slips or cards is encouraged. This creates a record if an investigator removes a file review, and makes retrieval of that file much easier.

SECURING INVESTIGATIVE INFORMATION

Considering the fact that many of the items under investigation are merely unproven allegations, the security of investigative files is critical. Lives and careers can and have been ruined because of leaks in filing systems. This information must therefore be kept strictly confidential, and the process of securing classified information and documents used by the military can be applied to investigative documentation. This military system of safeguarding classified and/or sensitive information is concerned with three aspects: clearance, access, and need to know.

Clearance refers to permitting only selected and screened personnel to view and work with selected material. In the military, background investigations are conducted and security clearances are granted. These can range from confidential to secret to top secret and beyond. Only persons with the appropriate clearance levels are permitted to work with and/or view classified material, and then only to the level that their clearance permits. This concept applies in our profession as well. For most investigative documentation, the only persons cleared to work with and/or view the material would be those personnel assigned to investigative duties. For some very sensitive information, only selected persons from within the investigative unit might be able to view and/or work with the documents. In the event that someone not assigned to the unit just wants "a look see" at the documents, their request should be denied.

Access refers to physical access. Information can only be protected if we control access to it. In the military, armed guards, barbed wire, motion detectors, locked doors, and other security systems are there to limit access to certain information. In the police profession, locked filing cabinets, password-protected computer systems, and similar safeguards are in place to protect documents and data.

Need to know refers to the fact that a person needs more than clearance and access to view and/or work with a file. They must also have a legitimate need to know. Nearly every failure of classified information security in recent years has been because of this element.

Background investigations, internal investigations, and allegations involving prominent persons are just a few files that may fall under this classification. In these cases, only those investigative personnel who actually are involved in the matters under investigation have a legitimate need to know.

INVESTIGATIVE PLANNING

When an experienced investigator begins a routine investigation, he or she generally spends little time planning. He or she just goes out and conducts the investigation. On the other hand, new personnel don't have the ability to conduct business in this manner. They need to identify the tasks to be done and a timetable in which to complete those tasks. They must take the time to review the initial report (in the case of reactive investigations) or review the intelligence information received (in the case of proactive investigations) and then plan their investigations. One method of ensuring that these investigations are actually planned is to require that the investigator submit a written investigative plan, no matter how simple the investigation might seem. A mandatory investigative plan forces personnel to think logically and in detail–often in a chronological manner–the steps to be taken. The investigative plan should include very clear instructions for completion. (See the example provided in Appendix 10.)

These written investigative plans, however, are not only useful for new investigators. They can also be used with less-than-stellar performers to make certain they conduct investigations in a thorough and professional manner. You can also use these plans as motivational tools. After a few weeks of having to complete these plans, some lessthan-stellar performers may voluntarily come to you with a list of ideas they developed on their own about how to proceed with a follow-up investigation. I have used investigative plans in this manner with some success. Although this doesn't always work, it's worth trying.

CASE REVIEW

Many investigative supervisors and managers consider case review as an undesirable task that should only be conducted when the case is being closed. In reality, nothing could be further from the truth. Case review must be an *ongoing process*, rather than a *single event*, which begins when the case is opened and ends when the case is closed. The reasons for conducting case review are as follows:

- **Confirms the work is being done.** Whenever I mention this, I get a number of investigative managers who immediately assume that I don't trust anyone to do their job, which is not true. Any investigative manager who has gone to a file that has been open for two weeks and contains one piece of paper (the original field report by patrol) knows what I mean. This is very similar to disciplinary matters: If it isn't on paper, it didn't happen. If you haven't seen the report on the interview, you can't know for certain that it was done. I have had the privilege of working with some of the finest investigators anywhere, and I still wanted concrete assurance that the work was being done. The only way to conclusively confirm this is by reviewing the case.
- **Assures accountability for the investigator's time.** Considering investigators have a great deal of autonomy, they must be expected to conduct their investigations in a thorough, professional manner with a minimum of close personal supervision. Case review is a mechanism for making certain that their time is

well spent and that the investigation is being conducted in an expeditious manner. It also provides helpful input for performance evaluations, because it is a good indicator of time management skills.

- **Ensures completeness of reporting.** By reviewing ongoing cases, you can make certain that the investigation is being *reported* in a complete and thorough manner.
- **Keeps you abreast of progress.** Without an ongoing case review process, you have no real idea of how the case is going. Simply talking to an investigator in passing is not the ideal way to stay abreast of the progress of any investigation. Regularly conducted case review is the only real way of staying on top of the work being conducted by investigators. This also gives you the opportunity to provide advice or guidance to the investigators who are lost or to mandate corrective action if the investigation is not being conducted in a complete and thorough manner.
- **Aids in the proper expenditure of resources.** An ongoing process of case review helps you with personnel allocation. If you regularly review cases, you may be able to determine whether a case needs additional investigators or whether too many investigators are working it. Making those determinations goes a long way to ensure you are using your most important resources wisely.
- **Identifies training needs.** If an investigator needs assistance in report preparation, report writing, investigative techniques, or any other matter, you can often identify these needs during case review. Without case review, these training needs may not be identified, and the investigator may go on repeating the same mistakes over and over.
- **Provides a means of answering inquiries on the investigation.** It has always been my experience that the most common time to receive an inquiry about a case from upper management, political officials, or the media is about 4:30 PM on a Friday afternoon, immediately preceding a 3-day holiday weekend. A regularly scheduled case review process will give you the information you need to address these inquiries in an intelligent and expeditious manner.

How to Conduct a Case Review

The case review process itself is not that difficult or mysterious. It consists of three main steps:

1. **Examine the reports as they come in.** Most investigative units have some type of report review in place, which is the first step in the case review process. Reading the reports lets you get a grasp on how the investigation is being conducted. You can check the timeliness and thoroughness of reporting and whether or not legal requirements are being met. You can also check items such as spelling and grammar. However, you can't make examination of reports the only element of the case review process. Most investigative managers have reports coming in from several investigators, each of whom is working on several investigations. It is virtually impossible to keep up with each and every one of these investigations by simply examining the reports as they are written.

2. **Discuss the case with the investigators.** Sitting down with the investigator and discussing the case can answer questions that cannot be answered by simply examining reports. Questions relating to the need for additional investigative resources on a particular investigation, how long the investigation needs to remain open if there are no additional leads to pursue, whether or not specialized equipment or outside agencies are needed, and other questions can only be answered by actually discussing the case with the investigators assigned.

3. **Discuss cases with prosecutors.** By querying prosecutors on a regular basis regarding a sampling of cases, you can learn first-hand how well your unit's work is contributing to the prosecution. This gives you the opportunity to identify and recognize the outstanding work of investigators and prosecutors. Or you may be able to identify shortcomings that can be addressed through additional or remedial training. In either case, both prosecutors and investigators will benefit from this interaction.

That last point needs expansion. Police, as a rule, don't like outsiders telling them how to do their jobs. Bringing prosecutors into the case review process should not be viewed as giving them an opportunity to direct the investigation or to second-guess the investigators. Rather, it should be viewed as giving another member of the investigative/prosecution team access to the process.

Clearly, the investigation and prosecution of criminal offenses is a team effort. Police can't prosecute offenders, and prosecutors can't investigate crimes. The talents and skills of both elements are critical in reaching the ultimate goal: the successful prosecution of guilty offenders. Investigators and investigative managers who don't believe in this team aspect are missing out on great opportunities to do their jobs better. Opening the case review process to prosecutors opens lines of communication. It can also help ensure compliance with legal procedures that can seriously hurt prosecutions if they are not observed. If you feel that dispositions on specific cases are not adequate or appropriate, discuss these specific cases with the prosecutor as soon as possible. If you don't, investigators will assume that the fault for the poor disposition lies squarely with the prosecutor, which may or may not be accurate.

I can recall one particular case in which a deputy sheriff (courtroom bailiff) was arrested and charged with molesting his girlfriend's 5-year-old daughter. The child sexual exploitation investigator assigned was a female who not only had a great deal of talent but was also a mother herself. This investigator took the case very seriously and did an outstanding job. The case was dismissed at the preliminary hearing, however, and the investigator was (understandably) furious. She immediately began a tirade on the prosecutor who had dismissed the case, calling him incompetent and inferring that the case had somehow been "fixed" due to the offender's position. Rumors such as this can seriously hurt the relationship between the police and prosecutors, and this issue needed to be addressed immediately. I scheduled a meeting with the supervisor of the prosecutor involved in the dismissal. During the meeting, I discovered that the dismissal had nothing whatsoever to do with the position of the offender but rather to the defense counsel insisting that the 5-year-old be examined in open court. (Thankfully, the court procedures have changed so that this is not always necessary.) The defense counsel indicated that during his cross-examination he would "destroy" the child on the stand. The prosecutor was faced with the possibility of having the child victim psychologically traumatized by this defense counsel, probably worse than during the offense itself. The decision was made to dismiss the case rather than risk further trauma to the victim.

I've always made it a practice to not second-guess other police offi-cers, and I have often extended that practice to prosecutors, as I did in this case. The prosecutor had a very difficult decision to make and apparently thought he was doing the right thing for the victim. When the actual facts of the matter and reasons for the dismissal were clear-ly explained to the investigator, she was still furious, but her fury was now (justifiably) directed at the defense counsel and not the prosecu-tor.

When to Conduct Case Review

Case review should be conducted on a regularly scheduled periodic basis. You should set a time frame during which you will conduct a review of all cases assigned to a particular investigator. It is much better to set spe-cific dates than to conduct case review on a flexible schedule. The problem with "flexible" is that it often translates to "never." Some investigative managers feel that a 30-day schedule is adequate and rotate the case review of their investigators so that each investigator goes through a formal review of assigned cases once during that peri-od. For example, in an investigative unit consisting of eight investiga-tors, case reviews could be conducted every Friday for two of the investigators. This would not be cumbersome because the reviews have a regular schedule and all personnel have plenty of time to pre-pare.

Periodic case review can be done in two formats: in the old-fash-ioned manner or by computer. In the old-fashioned method, you set up a three-ring binder with a divider for each investigator. A case review document is developed for each case assigned to an investiga-tor. (See the example provided in Appendix 11.) Periodic case review can be also done using a computer. Perhaps the easiest method of computerizing case review is to use a word processing program. Each investigator is assigned a folder and a file is opened for each case. Although database programs are also useful for computerized case review, most investigative managers are very familiar with navigating word processing programs. (See the example provided in Appendix 12.) The comments section might include information such as, "At the conclusion of the interview of John Doe, if negative, the investigator will recommend closing the case due to lack of leads." This places the impetus for action on the investigator. It also lets you set parameters on investigations rather than allowing them to remain open indefinitely.

The idea of computerized case review has come a long way in the past several years. Software programs that are used for case review have been developed in such a manner as to make the entire process much faster for both the investigative manager and the investigator assigned to the case. There are some elements of case review, however, that may not be adequately addressed, or that may be overlooked by the investigative manager who relies solely on computerized case review.

In the section above on "how to conduct case review" the idea of actually discussing the case with the investigator assigned is one of those things that can easily be overlooked when relying on computerized case review. This should be avoided, as it can prove very detrimental to the investigative unit. Actually sitting down and having a case review discussion with the investigator assigned can provide information on the progress of the case that cannot be gleaned from the computerized review. The little nuances of the investigation, which can guide management decisions, can better be learned through a discussion with the assigned investigator.

As an example, the investigator may feel that if he or she conducts two more interviews they will have enough to make an arrest or recommend closing of the case. This type of information probably cannot be learned from conducting a strictly computerized review, and the ramifications of the information can have an impact on that investigator's caseload, and the overall workings of the investigative unit.

Case review should be conducted when significant events occur. Events such as arrest of the offender, execution of a search warrant, or discovery of additional victims are all events that will trigger media interest and/or inquiries about the investigation. In order to be on top of the investigation, you should conduct a short case review at these critical events. This can be an abbreviated review, but it needs to include an examination of the investigative reports to ensure completeness as well as a discussion with the investigator so you are cognizant of significant aspects of the case that have occurred since the last periodic review.

Case review should be conducted before referral or closing of the case. This will provide you assurance that the investigation has been thoroughly and professionally concluded, and that the work product leaving the investigative unit has been professionally prepared. This final review is critical, so that cases referred for prosecution can assist in the most effective prosecution possible, and so that cases referred to another agency can be followed up effectively. If the case is closed without prosecution, it is critical for you to know that all possible investigative steps have been taken before closing. If this is not done, the investigative unit may be subject to extensive criticism by persons or organizations not pleased that the case is being closed without being referred for prosecution. Case review at this time may provide you with enough information to answer and/or deflect these inquiries and criticism.

CASE STATUS

The status of cases is an internal administrative device to assist in case management and control. Many agencies use simple designations:

- **Open.** The case is assigned to an officer and an investigation is actively being conducted. This doesn't necessarily mean on a daily basis, but investigative efforts are ongoing.
- **Suspended.** All available leads have been exhausted but the case has not been brought to a conclusion and investigative efforts may be resumed. This status is often used for serious offenses such as murder. The understanding is that no real progress is being made but the investigation may recommence if additional leads develop in the future.
- **Closed.** The case has been concluded, through referral for prosecution or referral to another agency.

The criteria for suspending investigative efforts should be written, and they should be the subject of supervisory/command review. Allowing investigators to be the sole determinants of when a case is closed or suspended is not a good idea, particularly in our media-driven society where second-guessing the police seems to be a national pastime. Without a well-defined, documented process, agencies open themselves to extensive criticism when unsolved cases are placed in suspended status or are closed. The criteria for closing or suspending investigative efforts often involve applying solvability and degree-of seriousness factors. These criteria may include:

- **Lack of further leads or solvability factors.** This must be carefully examined and clearly determined.
- **Unavailability of investigative resources.** Perhaps a case involves some specialized technique that would be too expensive or time consuming when compared to the seriousness of the offense. For example, you probably wouldn't seek DNA from a blood sample in a garage burglary when the item taken was a 15-year-old, unidentifiable lawn mower.
- **Insufficient degree of seriousness.** The case may involve some very minor allegations or no harm to a victim. Expending investigative personnel for such a case may be deemed irresponsible.

Sitting down with the victim of a crime and explaining that your decision to close out (or not to assign) an investigation is much more likely to be a positive experience if you are able to clearly explain that the criteria for case closing (or case assignment) are based on an objective appraisal of the facts, and that the same objective appraisal is applied to every case. This will demonstrate consistency, professionalism, and a lack of discrimination as it relates to the decision-making process. Without the ability to clearly explain the process, you are opening yourself (and your agency) to claims that the crime victim was somehow treated differently from other crime victims when the decision to close (or not assign) was made.

This has been a lengthy chapter and a seemingly lengthy process, but consider this: Investigative managers who conduct professional case management are better informed regarding the work of their investigators and are more able to make appropriate personnel allocation decisions. In other words, these managers are *managing* cases.

Chapter 10

MANAGING CONFIDENTIAL
SOURCE PROGRAMS

As a young investigator attending my first investigative training academy class, I recall an instructor at the academy who warned us that the Three B's would ruin our careers. The "Three B's" to which he was referring were "Booze, Bucks, and Babes." Although the reference to women as babes was (and still is) obviously inappropriate, these were the days before there were a large number of women officers. What the instructor was trying to get across was that problems associated with alcohol abuse, money issues (such as corruption, bribery, etc.), or issues regarding sexual indiscretions could ruin an officer's career.

While it's true that I have seen many cops ruin their careers by inappropriate conduct regarding alcohol, money, or sexual issues, there is a fourth item that I have seen destroy as many careers as I have the other three. That issue is the improper utilization of confidential sources of information, or C/S. The saddest part of this problem is that it seems that the officers most likely to have problems associated with C/Ss are those who are the most aggressive officers. Seldom do nonaggressive Officers have issues or problems with C/Ss, because they seldom utilize them. Those Officers who routinely utilize C/Ss unfortunately are at the greatest risk of having problems associated with their use.

Like any other issue dealing with unethical or misconduct by police, however, these problems are both identifiable and preventable. In order for these issues to be preventable, the agency must be serious about their views on the proper recruitment, utilization, and management of C/S programs. In order for these issues to be identifiable, the agency must have mechanisms in place that monitor the conduct of the officers working with C/Ss and the conduct of the C/Ss themselves. Without these mechanisms, the agency whose officers utilize C/Ss is sitting on a time bomb that is waiting to go off.

We have all seen accounts of police officers at the municipal, county, and state levels, as well as Federal Agents from many agencies that have ruined their careers, and in some cases gone to prison, for mishandling confidential sources. I have seen these things happen to police personnel whom I have known, and have read about and researched many other situations involving people whom I don't know. In observing these situations and while conducting research into similar situations, two things have struck me:

1. In most of these cases the agency had a sound policy in place to prevent the type of things that occurred. Simply having the policy in place, however, is meaningless unless the policy is enforced and unless personnel know that the agency is serious about it in all cases.
2. In many of these cases the investigative manager should have known that something in violation of the agency policy was occurring. Sometimes the investigative manager chose to ignore the problems for fear of "stifling" the imagination or performance of the investigator involved. In some cases, however, the supervisor was actually involved in the policy violations that led to the misuse of the confidential source.

Hopefully the information contained in this chapter will provide the investigator and the investigative manager with the tools to avoid any negative issues regarding C/Ss.

BASIC INFORMATION ON CONFIDENTIAL SOURCES

One of the most important and valuable aspects of investigative work is the ability to recognize, recruit, cultivate, and utilize confidential sources of information (C/Ss). Although we like to tell the media and the public that all of our cases are solved by a combination of "brilliant investigative work and dogged determination," the bottom line is that many cases are solved because somebody provided information to the police. In many of these instances, the information received by the police has come from a C/S.

The management of C/Ss can be one of the most difficult things for an investigative supervisor to control, and it has the potential for embarrassment to the investigator and the investigative manager, to the department, and to our profession. The problems that can arise from the undisciplined and unplanned utilization of C/Ss can be major in scope and potential effects. Managing investigative personnel that utilize C/Ss is one of the most difficult duties for the investigative manager. Cases have been overturned, guilty offenders have been released, police officers and C/Ss have been prosecuted and gone to prison, and lives, families, and careers have been destroyed. The sad part is that if some very simple and basic rules are strictly followed none of these things need occur.

Whether they are referred to as a Confidential Source (C/S), Cooperating Witness (C/W), Source of Information (SOI), Cooperating Individual (C/I) or whatever, these are *people who provide information to law enforcement regarding criminal activity.* For our purposes, we'll refer to a Confidential Source as a C/S.

It is critical that all investigators be taught to recognize the need for C/Ss in investigative work, which is probably something they haven't been exposed to or had to consider in patrol assignments. We must keep in mind that many newer investigators might never have had contact with a C/S, and can easily be led down the wrong path by a street-smart C/S. Although investigative personnel must be trained and encouraged to recognize, recruit, cultivate, and utilize C/Ss, they must also be schooled in the proper methods to be utilized. If we want them to avoid problems inherent with utilizing C/Ss we must have adequate policies in place and we must provide them with adequate training to do so.

The key to success when dealing with C/Ss is that the interactions must be totally professional, well disciplined, and conducted according to policy. Although C/Ss are very useful in investigating crimes of almost any type, problems usually occur when one of the following are allowed to occur:

Lack of control over the activities of investigative personnel who are interacting with C/Ss. Many investigators are very protective of their C/Ss, to the point where they will go to great lengths to protect their C/Ss, which sometimes can include hiding them from their supervisors, other officers, and anyone else who might steal them. Although this might sound very noble, and in some cases it is, the problems usually begin when the interactions between the C/S and the investigator are permitted to go beyond the bounds of "protecting them." In the event that investigators are interacting with C/Ss, it is the ultimate responsibility of the investigative manager to see to it that those interactions are being professionally conducted. Over the years, I've seen many situations in which investigators have gotten into serious trouble due to their interactions with C/Ss, and in most of those cases their supervisor either had no idea what was going on or knew what was going on and allowed it to continue.

Lest anyone think that this phenomenon is restricted to local, county, or state law enforcement agencies, in a recent situation in Boston, FBI Special Agent John Connolly was sentenced to 10 years in prison for (according to the Boston media) "allowing his C/Ss to run wild in the streets." This FBI agent had been utilizing two of Boston's most infamous organized crime figures as C/Ss, and during the time that he was using them they were allegedly responsible for more than 20 murders. Although the FBI claimed that Connolly was a "rogue" agent, working these C/Ss without the knowledge or consent of FBI headquarters, documents were introduced as evidence that revealed that FBI headquarters was aware of the use of these individuals. These documents also revealed that FBI headquarters not only condoned their use, but congratulated the efforts of Connolly for the cases made utilizing these C/Ss. Among the allegations against Connolly, it was alleged that he had provided information to his C/Ss (both of whom he had grown up with) regarding their criminal "competition."

For more information on this incident, I would highly recommend the book *Black Mass: The True Story of an Unholy Alliance Between the FBI and the Irish Mob* written by Dick Lehr and Gerard O'Neill.

At some point, someone should have stepped in and perhaps taken a closer review of exactly what was going on between Connolly and his childhood friends, to determine if in fact the policy on interacting with C/Ss was being followed and if the relationships were being maintained on a strictly professional basis. It would appear this was not done. However, it's not just the Feds that are subject to this type of problem. In 2002, a 32-year Chicago police veteran, renowned for his expertise on street gangs, was brought up on administrative charges regarding mishandling of a C/S. The allegations included asking a prosecutor to reduce charges against the C/S in exchange for information on a murder that the officer had withheld from other investigators who were working the murder investigation. According to the charges, he kept to himself information that one of his C/Ss had regarding a murder so that his C/S, who had been charged with beating an elderly woman, could benefit from the information. He is also accused of failing to report that another investigator had a romantic relationship with the same C/S.

Lack of control systems regulating the use of C/Ss, or the lack of adherence to those controls. Any law enforcement agency that allows investigators to utilize and interact with C/Ss that does not have a written policy addressing this practice is truly courting disaster. The problem is, however, that although some agencies have extensive written policies regarding the use of C/Ss, some agencies don't insist that their personnel adhere to these policies. Some investigative managers take the "wink and a nod" approach to controlling their personnel's use of C/Ss, oftentimes with tragic results. Well-written and thorough policies are only valuable if personnel conform to those policies, as well as know that sanctions will be applied if these policies are ignored or violated. If the message is being given that these policies are there for window dressing and don't really mean anything, abuses in the manner in which investigators interact with their C/Ss will occur, often with devastating results.

In addition to a lack of control over the activities of law enforcement personnel interacting with C/Ss and a lack of control systems for handling C/Ss, a third element that can lead to disaster is that a *desire to "make the big case" (sometimes at any cost) can cloud one's supervisory judgment and lead to a lack of control over personnel or a lack of adherence to established policy.* Sometimes investigators get so caught up in their quest to catch the bad guy that they take actions contrary to their policy and that seem to defy common sense. As admirable as their desire to stop criminal activity might be, to knowingly violate policy cannot be condoned. However, this problem doesn't only involve investigators; it can also involve supervisory personnel. Sometimes the supervisor gets so caught up in wanting their subordinates to make the case that their own judgment gets clouded and they allow policy violations to occur lest they be perceived as stifling the work of the work of their subordinates.

In narcotics work, this phenomenon is often referred to as "kilo fever," which means that common sense, policy, and in some cases legal regulations are permitted to go out the window because of the desire to lock up the drug dealer. It didn't really matter what actual amount of narcotics was involved, the fact that the desire of the investigators to capture the offender was so intense that it not only clouded their judgment, but also clouded the judgment of their supervisors. I've seen some otherwise competent personnel make somebody away some really bad decisions based on their desire to put somebody away.

Regardless of how much the offender desperately deserves to get locked up, it is obvious that investigative managers must still adhere to policies that govern the use of C/Ss and must still carefully monitor the activities of their personnel who are using them. The key to success when dealing with C/Ss is that the interactions must be totally professional, well disciplined, and conducted according to policy.

Prior to developing policies that govern the interaction of investigators working with C/Ss, or those policies aimed at administering the management of C/S programs, it is worthwhile to examine how these C/Ss are perceived by both the police and the public.

In the eyes of the public, C/Ss are considered weak and somewhat disgusting at best. From childhood we've all been cautioned against being a tattletale or squealer. Coming from a large family myself I can remember my sisters being rewarded for ratting out my brothers and I to our mother, while at the same time their being chastised for being tattletales and giving up their brothers. The names used by the public, authors, and the media to describe C/Ss are not necessarily terms of endearment either: squealer, rat, and stool are but a few. This feeling is exacerbated each time the public sees a C/S portrayed as some type of low life in the movies or on television. There was an old cop show called "Hill Street Blues," in which the commanding officer, Captain Frank Furillo, had a very highly placed C/S who was the leader of a Latino street gang. His name was Jesus, and many shows would end with Captain Furillo driving down a very dark alley, stopping at an entryway. A voice would come out of the shadows, provide Captain Furillo with the information to solve the crime of the week, and he'd drive away. The camera would remain fixed on the entryway, and soon the shadowy figure of Jesus the C/S would appear, looking like a cockroach emerging from darkness. I'm sure that the analogy wasn't wasted on the public watching the show.

A recent case in Chicago demonstrates the point of how C/Ss are perceived by the public even better. The FBI and U.S. Attorney's Office conducted a sting operation to obtain evidence against Chicago aldermen who were involved in shakedowns, bribery, and all sorts of chicanery. One of the aldermen, caught in the early stages of the investigation, agreed to wear a hidden transmitting device, commonly called a wire, against some of his fellow politicians. When some of his fellow aldermen (that he had helped catch) went to trial, of course the alderman who had been acting as a C/S had to testify and his identity and activities became public knowledge. When later interviewed on television regarding the turn of events, several aldermen made it very clear that their anger wasn't directed at their comrades who violated the public trust, but rather against the alderman who had ratted out his fellow aldermen by cooperating with the FBI and U.S. Attorney. As convoluted as this logic may seem, I think it speaks volumes about the attitude of the public toward the C/S (not to mention the sad commentary on the integrity of some public officials).

Unfortunately, with many police, the perception isn't really that much different. Police, as a rule, usually admire a "stand-up guy." When a criminal is caught and refuses to give up his friends and/or criminal cohorts, many cops think it somewhat noble that the person who did the crime is willing to do the time rather than cut a deal by providing information on their friends. Unfortunately, this sentiment can sometimes be carried to the extreme, particularly with regard to police corruption. If an officer involved in committing criminal acts is protected by fellow officers due to their desire not to be squealers, this is truly a sad state of affairs for our profession.

Some officers and even some investigators, have such feelings of disgust for a C/S who is willing to provide information (for whatever reason) that they refuse to work with them. I would submit that investigators who take this approach are causing themselves much more work and missing out on a number of opportunities to make good quality arrests. If an investigator feels this strongly about not wanting to have any contact with C/Ss, perhaps they'd be better off in a patrol assignment. Even if these feelings of disgust are there, the officer or investigator must put them aside, do what is needed to get the information from the C/S, and simply do his or her job.

WHERE DO CONFIDENTIAL SOURCES COME FROM?

Investigative personnel must be trained to recognize that virtually *any* interaction is a potential source of C/Ss. Unfortunately, however, this is seldom emphasized and as a result there are probably more investigators out there overlooking potential C/Ss than there are those who take the time to try and recruit them. The simple answer to the primary question of who can be a C/S, is *ANYONE! There are no entrance requirements.* C/Ss are not necessarily people who have extensive criminal records. What is important is that they have the information on criminal activity, or that they have the means available to locate the information. Particularly for newer investigators, there are several ready sources of C/S recruitment that are often overlooked. Those sources are their friends in patrol, who are out there interacting with the public 24 hours a day, and who come across a variety of people, including many potential sources of information. Newer investigators should make it a point to talk to their buddies in patrol and seek their assistance in recruiting new C/Ss. Every arrest, it should be explained, has the potential for a new C/S.

The problem with soliciting this type of assistance, however, is that the investigator must be ready and willing to actually respond to the calls from patrol officers. The first time that the Investigator refuses to come out at 3 a.m. to interview a potential C/S that has just been brought in by a patrol officer is probably the last time that Patrol Officer will make the effort to call him or her. When the investigator really understands that the potential really significant information is there in every interview, it can make getting out of bed at 3am a little more palatable. Patrol officers should be encouraged to be on the lookout for potential C/Ss. This should be made as simple as possible, so that they don't have to jump through a lot of hoops to initiate their recruitment efforts. One method of making it simple is to utilize a very simple document. This two-sided C/S Referral Card is roughly the size of a traffic citation, and several copies should be provided to each interested patrol officer. The reason for the size is that it allows the patrol officer to carry the forms in his or her citation book for ready access. The C/S Referral Card can be utilized to encourage patrol officers to recognize, cultivate, and refer potential C/Ss to the investigative unit. (See the example provided in Appendix 13.)

When the patrol officer comes across a potential source of information in situations that do not necessitate the immediate call out of an investigator, the card is filled out and turned into the Investigations Unit along with a copy of the incident report or citations. The referral card and report is then reviewed by investigators who then schedule a debriefing with the potential C/S. The card itself is very self-explanatory, in that it requires not only complete identifiers of the potential C/S, it also includes information regarding how to contact the person, gang affiliation, prior criminal history, and current charges. The card is designed for the patrol officer who has no background in recruiting a C/S. The patrol officer is instructed to *"inform the arrestee (potential C/S) that it is possible to receive leniency or consideration on their current charges in exchange for providing information."* It also makes it very clear that *"no explicit or implicit promises can be made by the Patrol Officer regarding disposition of pending charges."* The Patrol Officer simply conducts the interview, completes and refers the form, accompanied by their field report, to the investigative unit. An investigator is assigned to follow up on the contact, and attempt to recruit the person as a working C/S.

There is a basic premise in psychology that behavior that is rewarded will increase in frequency. If this is true, and I believe that it is, then if patrol officers are somehow rewarded for referring potential C/Ss to the Investigative Unit then these occurrences will increase in frequency. When a patrol officer refers a potential C/S who provides information that leads to a search warrant, for example, the patrol officer who initially made the referral should be invited to come along on the search warrant execution. In addition, a memorandum of appreciation of some sort should definitely be presented to the patrol officer and a copy should be placed in their personnel file. Patrol officers who routinely go the extra mile and refer potential C/Ss to Investigations need to have that information known so that their efforts can be taken into consideration in the event that they apply for future openings in the Investigations Unit.

It is amazing how much a little bit of positive reinforcement, such as being invited to go out on a tactical operation and receiving a "happy-gram" in a personnel file can motivate some patrol officers. I can recall a patrol officer who made a traffic stop that led to an arrest for possession of a stolen motor vehicle. Rather than merely process the arrestee and move on, this patrol officer took the time to interview the person and complete a Confidential Source Referral Card. The arrestee became a very active C/S, and the patrol officer got to accompany Investigators on numerous Search Warrant executions and arrests resulting from this C/S's information. Each time that this Patrol Officer came across someone with even a little bit of potential, an interview was conducted and the person was referred. While only a small percentage of those referred actually became C/Ss, the Patrol Officer's initiative was admirable. That Patrol Officer is now assigned to Investigations, working as a supervisor in a multi-agency Major Crime Task Force. This type of initiative, if properly recognized, will lead to more and more similar displays of initiative. Besides obtaining referrals of potential C/Ss from patrol, there are several other sources for these important investigative assets, of which investigators should be aware. These include "flipping" defendants, walk-ins, outside agency referrals, having a good reputation, and friends and associates of defendants.

Flipping" Defendants

This is perhaps the most common source for a C/S. It occurs when someone is arrested for an offense and is then convinced to cooperate with police in order to lessen the penalty that they will receive for their original offense. Individuals who have committed a variety of offenses have taken advantage of this situation and have provided some very valuable information. Defendants that "flip" (often called "flippers") range from the young person caught shoplifting who provides information regarding the local small-time dope dealer to people like Sammy "The Bull" Gravano, an associate of (former) organized crime figure John Gotti, who provided enough information on the former "Teflon Don" to get him put away.

Caution must be taken, however, that the aggressive investigator is very careful in their approach to the potential "flipper." *No promises of leniency can be made.* The only promise that can legitimately be made is that the cooperation of the C/S will be brought to the attention of the prosecutor. On many occasions, the attorney representing the C/S will want to get involved in the negotiations for leniency on current charges. In these cases the attorney usually meets with the prosecutor and the police in order to provide, in very generic terms, the information the C/S possesses, and to find out what is being offered in terms of leniency. This information is occasionally later provided in written form called a proffer. Once the agreement is made, the C/S provides the information and the investigators make their case(s). Investigators should not make the assumption that only offenders facing serious charges are potential "flippers." The opposite is true, in that many very valuable C/Ss have provided information in exchange for leniency on such mundane charges as traffic offenses. In my own experience, some of the best C/Ss I've seen were performing their services for something as seemingly mundane as getting their driver's licenses returned after suspension or revocation.

Walk-ins

Investigators should be encouraged to view almost any interaction as a potential source for C/Ss, and people who voluntarily walk-in to police to provide information should not be overlooked. They can sometimes provide very valuable information. The reasons for these types of people providing information will be examined when motivations are discussed. Included in this category are anonymous calls to police from people providing information. Although it is true that any information received from an anonymous caller must be carefully scrutinized and corroborated, even this type of information should be taken seriously.

I can recall one former C/S relationship that started out with an anonymous call. The caller had gotten my name from an unknown source and called to inform me that he was working as a truck driver for an auto parts company that he suspected was involved in "chopping" stolen cars. He would not provide me with a name or any identifiers, nor would he provide me with the name of the company for whom he worked. I offered to take his information anyway, and this led to a series of calls over the next few months in which he provided me with a great deal of virtually useless information. I kept asking for vehicle identification numbers so that I could identify stolen vehicles, and he kept providing me with stock numbers, inventory numbers, and part numbers, none of which were helpful. After several phone calls, he finally agreed to meet with me in person. Following our meeting, he provided information that led to several cases and arrests, including auto theft, narcotics, and even a shooting. Not too bad a result from an anonymous caller.

Outside Agency Referrals

Another excellent source for C/Ss are referrals from fellow law enforcement personnel. Often a potential C/S does not possess information regarding crime in one community, but does have information regarding criminal activity in another community. This is particularly true in the maze of overlapping suburbs surrounding large urban areas, where police jurisdictions often result in many contiguous community boundaries. Effective liaisons between investigators, which should be encouraged by the investigative manager, can sometimes lead to very valuable C/Ss and some excellent cases.

I was once approached by a municipal P.D. patrol officer who had stopped an individual for a traffic violation only to find that the driver was driving on a revoked driver's license. The driver was arrested and taken to the station for processing. As they began talking at the station, the driver made it clear that he was willing to help in any way possible to avoid the arrest and to get his driver's license back. The patrol officer called me and together we interviewed this potential C/S. This man had no criminal record and his only motivation for offering to assist the police was a desire to get his revoked driver's license back. This initial interview led to several arrests for major felony offenses, uncovered a theft ring involving a supervisor with the U.S. postal system, and the recovery of several stolen U.S. Treasury checks. And all of this started with a traffic stop by an excellent patrol officer from a six-person police department.

Hard Work and a Good Reputation

Although it might sound rather trite, a very valuable source for potential C/Ss is simply having a good reputation on the street. Criminals know which investigators can be trusted to keep their word and which will take advantage of them. Investigators who acquire a reputation for treating people fairly, keeping their word, and being honest can sometimes have potential C/Ss seek them out. It is the job of the investigative manager to make certain that investigators are aware of this potential, and to encourage the type of behavior that helps achieve such a reputation. This type of reputation not only results in some chances for potential C/Ss, but can make one's job a great deal easier overall.

Friends and Associates of Defendants

This is usually totally overlooked as a potential source of C/Ss. This avenue is available to investigators when the potential C/S is unable to provide any useful information themselves. They must be convinced that they must know somebody who can provide information, perhaps a relative, friend, or criminal associate who could provide some information to the police. The selling point here is that any cases that are based on information provided by their relative, friend, or criminal associate will be credited to them to the extent that information on their cooperative efforts will be provided to prosecutors.

Another very common situation in which the friends and associates of a potential C/S might be of benefit is when the potential C/S is jailed on a charge and the bond set is too high for him or her to be released. In this instance, the potential C/S must be convinced to contact a friend, relative, or criminal associate and to convince them to work with the police. Once again, the selling point is that any cases that are based on information provided by their relative, friend, or criminal associate will be credited to them, and that the extent of their cooperative efforts will be provided to prosecutors.

DETERRENTS TO COOPERATION

Convincing people, particularly criminals, to willingly provide information and work with the police in catching other criminals is not an easy task. There are several deterrents to someone being willing to assist the police as a C/S. Some of these deterrents are so basic that they are extremely difficult to overcome, such as public sentiment, fear of reprisals, stigmatization personal pride, or mistrust of police.

Public Sentiment

Many people, particularly criminals, are reluctant to assist police as a C/S because they think they will be looked down on by their friends and associates. This probably stems from the distaste for tattletales that most of us hear about in our youth. As stated earlier, the general view of the public toward the C/S is hardly positive, and just the fact that they will be viewed negatively is enough to dissuade many people from wanting to assist the police.

Fear of Reprisals

This is perhaps the most significant deterrent. People are genuinely afraid of what will happen to them if it becomes known that they are in fact cooperating as a C/S with the police. There are countless stories of people being found murdered after it became known that they were acting as C/Ss for the police.

Among the more illustrative anecdotes is how the suspected C/S is often treated by the Irish Republican Army, a process known as kneecapping. The suspected informer (or quisling as they are known in Ireland) is held down and a large auger bit is drilled into his or her patella (kneecap). The person operating the drill must be somewhat skilled so as to not go too deep and puncture the popliteal artery, a major blood vessel. Instead the patella is drilled only deep enough to cause a permanent limp when the victim recovers. The purpose of the exercise is that the person now becomes a "walking testimonial" about what happens to informers who dare to cooperate with "the enemy." As a matter a fact, there's an Irish poem that carries the line "and let them [the quislings] be known for their limping." I would personally see this as an extremely effective deterrent to informing.

Everyone has heard of the famed Colombian Necktie, where the throat of the suspected C'S is slit and his or her tongue is pulled out through the slit. You can imagine the deterrent effect against cooperating with the police on anyone who finds a body in this condition.

The shock value of these heinous acts is designed to serve one purpose-to preclude anyone who is even contemplating assisting the authorities to think long and hard before they do so. And yet, people continue to provide information to the police. It's up to the investigator to determine what the potential C/S fears most-reprisals from the criminal element or punishment for their misdeeds.

Stigmatization

When it becomes known that someone has cooperated with the police as a C/S, particularly if it is in an open forum, as is the case if they have to testify in court, they are often stigmatized for life. Their potential for a successful future as a criminal is dramatically diminished as they are branded as an informer, someone never to be trusted again. For the career criminal, this is a virtual death sentence of sorts, in that their livelihood is impacted. Many career criminals have absolutely no desire whatsoever for anything even close to the straight life as a law-abiding citizen. They practice their criminal trade for their entire lives, cognizant of the risks and consequences, but apparently happy in the freedom that the criminal lifestyle provides. For them to risk this freedom by becoming stigmatized as a turncoat to their criminal associates is quite a deterrent to overcome. For the noncareer criminal, they still have to put up with the sneers and jeers of the public and their friends, many of whom will never trust them, and will probably always wonder "if it came down to it, would this person turn me in for something that I did?"

Personal Pride

Some people are reluctant to cooperate with police based on their distaste for the whole idea. These people seem to have a somewhat convoluted sense of honor that allows them to justify someone engaging in illegal or unethical behavior as somehow being a better person than the individual that turns them into authorities.

Mistrust of Police

This is a major deterrent to cooperation with the police. Unfortunately, we as police often bring this mistrust on ourselves. Officers, particularly investigators, who routinely lie to people, and who seem to take pleasure in this type of conduct give the rest of us a very bad reputation to overcome. Seldom if ever are these types of investigators the recipients of walk-in C/Ss, who are usually motivated to seek out police based on their reputation for fairness and honesty. Although our main goal is to lock up the bad guys, how we do it is what makes (or breaks) our personal reputations. Being straightforward with people, including the criminals who we investigate, is usually a good business practice. It can sometimes pay dividends for us when they trust us enough to cooperate and provide us with information. As many deterrents as there are, the talented and skillful investigator can often overcome them by using their imagination and pushing the right buttons, particularly during their initial contact with the potential C/S.

DETERMINING MOTIVATIONS

After understanding the various deterrents that would present someone from providing information to the police as a C/S, it is equally important that investigators learn to determine what would motivate an individual to assist police by providing information, possibly on their friends or criminal associates. Determining what motivates the potential C/S is critical for the investigator to obtain the best information possible. This is particularly critical if it is anticipated or possible that undercover personnel will be introduced to criminals by the C/S at some later date.

Some of the most common motivators include:

Fear

This can mean fear of punishment, fear of associates, or fear of the police, all of which are valuable motivators from our perspective. Fear is the most common motivator, and can be successfully played upon, even with the most hardened of criminals. Do you really suppose that Sammy "The Bull" Gravano would have cooperated with the police if he wasn't afraid of going to prison for a very long period?

In the event that the potential C/S is likely to be incarcerated, this fear can definitely be used as a motivator, particularly if the C/S has a family or some other reason for seriously fearing being locked up (such as fear for personal safety). I worked an investigation while undercover in which a very active truck and cartage thief was targeted. After the arrest and processing he was given an opportunity to "help himself out" by assisting the police, which he vehemently refused to do. He was convicted, did his time, and I never thought much of him until 10 years later when he was arrested as one of nearly 100 defendants from an undercover sting project that some of the investigators under my command had worked. During the processing, I stopped by the booking room to say hello as we were (in a manner of speaking) old friends. He immediately suspected why I was there and flatly refused to provide any assistance at all to the police, reminding me that he was always known as a stand-up guy, capable of doing his own time for his own crime. While we were spending some time catching up with each other's lives, he mentioned that he had married and had a little girl. After looking at her photo in his personal property I remarked that I too had a daughter, and went on and on about how much fun I was having watching my daughter grow up. I then told him that it was too bad that he wasn't going to get the chance (for at least the next 5–10 years) to watch his own daughter grow up, but I'm sure that she'd understand and probably forgive him when he got out of prison because after all, he was a "stand-up guy." It took approximately three weeks of being locked up on an extremely high bond that he was unable to make, but he eventually did call and offer to assist the investigator who had arrested him by making a telephone introduction to a cousin who turned out to be an excellent C/S.

Knowing which button to push to maximize the fear that the defendant is feeling is something that comes with experience, but knowing that fear can be a powerful motivator for many people is a good start. Prisons are very dangerous places, some of which have extensive networks of gangs among the inmates. It is completely natural for someone to fear being placed into that environment, and that fear can be manipulated (and perhaps exaggerated to some extent) by the investigator. People who are fearful of their criminal associates need to know that it is virtually impossible for police to protect them 24 hours a day. They also need to know that if they cooperate with police and the information is valuable enough, they may assist in putting the focus of their fear behind bars, or they may be eligible for a fresh start in some type of a witness protection program. These might be just the things that reluctant individuals might need to persuade them to voluntarily cooperate with police.

Revenge

This is probably the most dangerous motivation from the supervisory perspective, due to the fact that C/Ss motivated by revenge can cause some of the biggest problems and embarrassment for you and your agency. This desire for revenge against their enemies can be for either real or imagined wrongs, but what real difference does that make? Whether or not they were actually wronged by someone should be immaterial to the police; if their motivation is revenge against someone else, that information might be useful. The C/S motivated by revenge can have those feelings of revenge played on by a skilled investigator, but care must be taken not to go too far. The reason for this caution is that if the desire for revenge gets to be too powerful, the C/S's desire to satisfy his or her need for revenge might lead to exaggeration and possible problems such as entrapment, planting evidence, and so on, none of which we can tolerate. Knowing just how far to play on the revenge motivation is something that comes with experience, but knowing that it is possible can be very helpful.

The revenge motive is particularly strong when dealing with a jilted lover situation. There is no doubt in my mind that prisons all over the world contain a good number of residents, both male and female, who are there after having been turned in by a former lover or spouse that they have wronged in some way. I believe in the old axiom "Hell hath no fury like a woman scorned." It has been my experience that there are many "wronged" wives and girlfriends out there who have laid a great deal of fury on their former husbands or significant others. The same holds true for men, but perhaps not with the same frequency.

Revenge among (former) criminal associates is also a very strong motivation, but caution must be taken to properly school the C/S in the permissible and nonpermissible methods and techniques of working a case up on their intended target. Legal issues such as entrapment, as well as nefarious conduct such as planting evidence and providing false information, must be clearly explained and the C/S must be aware that these things will not be tolerated, no matter how bad they want the intended target arrested. Utilizing the anger of the C/S can be very problematic if it is not strictly monitored and controlled.

Mercenary

This refers to a C/S who is motivated by money. Many police departments and almost all investigative agencies have funds budgeted to allow for payments for information or for the undercover purchase of evidence. Some investigators find this practice of paying for information somewhat distasteful, and those investigators usually don't work too well with C/Ss. It is an unfortunate fact of life that all cases are not made on brilliant investigative work and dogged determination, but in fact, some of the best cases are made because of a paid C/S. Although payments to C/Ss by police can (and have) led to some very embarrassing situations, if administered properly, this is not necessarily the outcome. Most payments to a C/S are usually on a C.O.D. (Cash on Defendant) basis. In this payment scenario, the C/S is not paid until such time as they provide information that actually leads to an arrest or seizure, or for intelligence information that is valuable to the police.

Occasionally a C/S may be placed on a retainer, in which they are paid on a periodic basis (weekly, monthly, etc.) for information that they provide. This is a rare occurrence in my experience, perhaps because the C/S paid on a retainer basis might not be as active or aggressive as a C/S who only gets paid when they produce.

Perhaps the main problem with working a C/S that is motivated by mercenary motivations, whether they are paid C.O.D. or on a retainer, is that caution must be taken that they're not going to the highest bidder and involving other agencies in your operations without mentioning it to you. There have been many situations in which a C/S goes to a local agency and provides information for money, then goes to a county, state, or federal agency to "sell" the exact same information. Although I greatly admire the initiative and entrepreneurial spirit of a C/S who would engage in such behavior, I shudder to think what could happen when the arrest is about to take place and the police are unaware that other police are also involved. This scenario brings to mind the gunfight at the OK Corral, but in this case it involves police versus police, which is not a pleasant thought at all. The C/S who is going to be paid must be very carefully and thoroughly made aware of the agency's administrative regulations, such as registration, appropriate paperwork, signed receipts for funds received, and the like. and this should be done at the initial debriefing. Any agency that allows its investigators to pay any C/S any amount of money and does not have a written policy in place is, in my opinion, courting disaster. A model policy will be discussed further in the chapter on administrative considerations.

In addition to money that is specifically budgeted for payment of C/Ss, investigators should also consider using finder's fees and rewards from businesses and insurance companies to provide funding for C/Ss, but they need to be extremely careful that there is no appearance of impropriety on their part. Most insurance companies have funds budgeted and are willing to provide payment to recover the property that they have insured, and if an investigator has a C/S who can provide valuable information toward that end, they are usually willing to pay the C/S. I had a C/S that provided me with information regarding a stolen earth-moving machine similar to a huge bulldozer that was being used by a construction company in the Chicago area. After locating and recovering the machine, I contacted the insurance company who advised that they normally provided a "finder's fee reward" for such information. After clearly explaining that I myself was not soliciting the reward but that it was for a C/S they were very happy to provide the C/S with a check for their standard 10% of the value of the recovered property. Fortunately for this C/S, the machine was then currently valued at nearly $80,000, so he received a check for almost $8,000. This proved to be an excellent incentive for this C/S, who spent many days and nights looking for additional pieces of stolen heavy equipment.

Egotism

The C/S who is motivated by ego is often referred to as a cop freak or wannabe. These are often people who could not, for whatever reason be police officers. They sometimes figure that the next best thing to being a cop is hanging out with cops, and one way to do that while at the same time get into the good graces of cops, is to provide them information. While I don't have a real problem with that mode of thinking, I have personally seen some of the damage that this type of C/S has caused and tend to be extremely wary of them. Among the most difficult C/Ss to control, these C/Ss often magnify their own importance, apparently believing that they are in fact law enforcement officers. They often become too involved in the case activity, again based on their exaggerated view of their position. They don't seem to take direction very well, and have to be reminded of who is in charge on a regular basis. They have been known to identify themselves as police officers, which is a very good reason to dissuade your investigators from giving them their official agency business cards. They sometimes take "police action," such as making arrests or conducting searches, even though these are patently illegal. They can cause a great deal of embarrassment for the investigators working with them, for the investigative manager, and for your agency. Investigators must keep in mind that the actions of a C/S are going to be viewed as being the actions of an actual agent of law enforcement, and some courts are reluctant to accept the excuse that the C/S was acting independently when engaging in their misbehavior.

This is not to say that this type of C/S should never be worked, but it is important to maintain strict control over these individuals and to insist on strict adherence to established policy. The investigator must constantly weigh the potential value of this type of individual against their potential for embarrassment. When the scales begin to tip toward embarrassment instead of the potential value, it might be time to dismiss them and move on. The main problem that I have seen with this type of C/S is that they seem to have an absolutely uncanny ability to ingratiate themselves with the police. They hang around with the police, probably buying more than their share of drinks and/or meals. They are often able to provide some additional value to some investigators, such as romantic companionship or other things that should be avoided. They are able to walk on the edge of police life, getting involved in the criminal element at times, and working with the police at other times. Too often, these people, particularly when working with a newer or possibly somewhat naïve investigator, can completely take over the relationship, and begin to play the investigator like a violin, often with tragic results to the career of the investigator and to the agency involved.

Perverse Motivations

This refers to a C/S who is motivated by some perverse self-interest. They may be providing information in an effort to eliminate their competition. Although attempting to get rid of competition is done everyday in business, it is usually done by having sales, better service, or other incentives to consumers. With regard to the C/S motivated by perverse motivations, however, their ultimate goal may be to provide information leading to the arrest of criminals engaging in the exact same type of criminal activity in which they themselves are engaged. In this manner, their competition is gone and they are free to continue engaging in their criminal conduct unfettered. This is often based on a convoluted view of the concept of supply and demand, in that the product or service that they provide goes up in value if they can successfully eliminate their criminal competitors. If they're not actively providing information to police on their competitors in order to eliminate the competition, they may be attempting to divert suspicion from themselves by focusing police attention on their competitors. They sometimes believe that police are stupid enough to focus all of their attention on their competitors and forget all about them.

They may also be working with police in an effort to obtain other information, such as information on investigative procedures like how surveillances are conducted. This information would be very valuable and may provide them with the knowledge to avoid getting caught in the future. The unfortunate thing is that this sometimes works, as some police seem extremely willing to brag about how good they are at catching bad guys, even to other bad guys. Sometimes police don't stop and think that this C/S might be seeking this information not because he or she is so impressed with police as to be fascinated with how we work, but rather so that they can use the information against police in the future.

These C/Ss may be interacting with police in an effort to identify undercover police personnel, determine the locations used by police, or to determine which vehicles are being used by the police. There is also the chilling possibility that they may be interacting with the police in an effort to identify other C/Ss that are currently on the police payroll, which is an excellent reason why police should be extremely reluctant to provide any C/S with the identity of any other C/S. This knowledge would be worth a great deal, particularly to active criminal groups or organized crime enterprises. Unfortunately, this information could (and has) also been extremely dangerous to police, particularly undercover personnel. Some undercover personnel whose cover stories have been compromised have been killed or seriously injured due to the fact that their C/S was in fact collecting information against them for use by the criminal element. Can you imagine being an undercover officer who thinks that your cover story is intact when in fact it has already been compromised by a C/S?

There are other examples of surveillances and investigations being compromised, C/Ss or Officers being hurt or worse, and a great deal of investigative time and effort wasted due to the activities of this type of C/S. This is another reason why investigators should be repeatedly cautioned to *provide only the amount of information to their C/S as is absolutely necessary for them to operate.* Any excess information provided might come back to haunt them.

Personal Motivations

These C/Ss can be legitimately good citizens or even former criminals. They may be motivated by repentance, they can be people simply fed up with crime, or even someone out to right a wrong done to a family member or friend. Again, it is immaterial if this wrong really even occurred. Again, it is important that the investigator accurately determine the true motivation of the C/S. With this type of C/S, the true motivation is usually very clearly stated during the initial debriefing. Although as a rule these people will probably not have extremely valuable information as they are not usually connected to the criminal element, investigators shouldn't arbitrarily discount their value as a C/S.

Investigators must keep in mind that all C/Ss have some type of motivation, and many have multiple motivating factors. It is critical that these motivations be determined, and once they are determined the investigator must maintain the type of professional relationship with the C/S that will allow the investigator to remain in control regardless of the C/S's motivation. Without this control, the inherent danger of working with any C/S is exacerbated.

INITIAL DEBRIEFING AND BEGINNING THE RELATIONSHIP

My little Italian mother used to tell me that "you only get one chance to make a good first impression," and she was absolutely right. The same principle applies to the initial contact that the investigator has with the potential C/S. If it is planned and done correctly, the stage can be set for the receipt of some excellent information and perhaps a long and beneficial relationship. If it is not done correctly, it could lead to a relationship full of problems. It's up to the investigator to do it correctly, because there's only one chance.

The initial contact with the potential C/S will be either voluntary or involuntary. Voluntary contact is usually limited to walk-ins or referrals, while involuntary contacts usually occur with arrestees or other prisoners. In either case, a *face-to-face debriefing is essential.* You wouldn't conduct a key interview/interrogation of a main suspect in a murder investigation by mail or over the phone, and I would strongly recommend against allowing investigators to conduct the initial debriefing interview with a potential C/S any other way but in person. The reason that it must be conducted in person is that the initial debriefing will set the stage, not only for future meetings, but for the entire relationship.

The manner in which the investigator approaches the potential C/S during the initial debriefing is his or her one and only chance to make a very convincing impression. The investigator must be able to sell themselves as someone who is competent, professional, knowledgeable, discreet, and most important, someone who can be trusted. The mechanics of the interview such as language, attitude, and body language must be considered carefully and well planned, because the potential C/S will undoubtedly respond to these things, regardless of their motivation for assisting the police. No competent investigator would rush into a key interview/interrogation with a main suspect of a murder investigation, and no competent investigator should rush into the initial debriefing with a potential C/S. Several things are crucial for a successful debriefing:

The investigator must do his or her homework and prepare for the interview/debriefing. There are a couple of reasons that this is so important. First of all, the fact that the investigator has done his or her homework and prepared for the interview demonstrates to the potential C/S that they thought enough of this interview to prepare for it. Another reason is that by doing his or her homework they decrease the likelihood that the potential C/S is able to scam them with false or fictitious information. Without the prior knowledge that comes from doing one's homework, the streetwise C/S can play games with the investigator all day long. When doing the necessary homework, the investigator should consider any and all information on the potential C/S's criminal history, on their associates, their past conduct, and any current offenses. Having this information on hand is important because it will demonstrate to the potential C/S that the investigator is truly a professional who knows what he or she is doing. It is much more likely that this type of Investigator will instill the necessary confidence in the potential C/S for them to overcome the deterrents to cooperating with the police in the first place.

The investigator controls the interview. It is absolutely mandatory that the investigator, not the potential C/S, be in control of the interview. Controlling the interview is a direct result of the amount of planning that goes into the interview. Having all of the necessary documentation on hand is critical. If the investigator plans on making reference to the potential C/S's criminal history, for example, it would be a good idea to have the documentation available. If the investigator plans on discussing potential criminal targets that are associates of the potential C/S, it might be a good idea to have available police reports that show the relationship between the potential C/S and the criminal target. The investigator is the one asking the questions, and not the one providing information on how the agency operates. Having a plan on what is going to be discussed can prevent the interview from going off course and becoming merely a conversation. Having a plan for the interview and maintaining control is also important in that it sets the stage for the entire relationship between the investigator and the potential C/S. Having a plan also demonstrates to the potential C/S that he or she is dealing with someone who is a professional, which can make it less likely that the potential C/S will attempt to take control of the situation.

The investigator should not give out anymore information than is absolutely necessary. This is based on the concept of need to know, in which only as much information is provided as the recipient actually needs to know to complete the task at hand. As much time as necessary should be spent selling the confidentiality of your agency's C/S program, as this can be an incentive for potential C/Ss to cooperate.

Why would someone willingly cooperate with the police if they are not absolutely certain that the fact that they are cooperating will be kept strictly confidential? A clear explanation of the lengths that the agency goes to safeguard their identity and involvement might be what is needed to convince the reluctant potential C/S to actually cooperate. The procedures used in registering, paying, and protecting the identity of a C/S should be carefully explained. If the program is in fact sound and professionally managed, this information in and of itself can assist the investigator in convincing the potential C/S to provide information.

The investigator needs to do a thorough debriefing. This is sometimes an extremely difficult concept to get across to some investigators, particularly the specialists. Investigators who are specialists in some type of investigation sometimes get tunnel vision and are only concerned with their particular specialty. Although this may be beneficial during the everyday work efforts, it can be disastrous when it comes to the initial debriefings of potential C/Ss. Any investigators, whether they are specialists or generalists, must be willing to seek out *all information regarding any and all criminal activity* about which the potential C/S has information. I have actually seen a debriefing interview of a potential C/S by a narcotics investigator in which the potential C/S offered information on a burglary group and an auto thief, and that information was turned down and ignored by the Narc because it didn't have anything to do with narcotics. This is ridiculous, in that the information should have been obtained and turned over to other investigators that could work the information. Complete and thorough debriefings are the result of some essential elements:

- the investigator must recognize the importance of the potential information, regardless of what type of criminal activity is involved
- the investigator must have prepared well for the interview, ready to capitalize on whatever information is provided
- the investigator must be able to convince the potential C/S that they possess very important information that can greatly assist the police (as well as themselves).

The investigator must insist on specific and complete information. This is a critical element of the initial debriefing in that it sets the stage for later contacts, and actually trains the C/S for later operations. The potential C/S who is allowed to provide generic or vague information at the initial debriefing will continue to do so, even though the generic information that they are providing is virtually worthless. Can you imagine submitting a request for a search warrant to a judge in which the property is described as "probably the second or third house on the block, which might be green but possibly blue"? You'd be laughed out of the judge's chambers with this type of nondescript and generic information. Information such as names, addresses, license numbers, phone numbers, and so on needs to be received as accurately as possible. The investigator must carefully and thoroughly explain the necessity for thorough information. An explanation of how specific information is necessary for search warrant applications, requests for overhears, and the like will usually convince the C/S of the necessity for them to go the extra mile and obtain accurate information. If this is done correctly and insisted on at the initial debriefing, the C/S will usually provide specific and useable information for the duration of the working relationship.

ADMINISTRATIVE CONSIDERATIONS REGARDING CONFIDENTIAL SOURCES

Prior to insisting on the responsible cultivation, recruitment, and utilization of C/Ss by investigators, the system for handling the C/S must be in place and operational. Elements of that system must include registration, documentation of their activities, and a comprehensive payment policy. The reason for documentation and registration of C/Ss is to create a paper trail of the interactions between the police and the C/S.

The initial instructions from the investigator to the C/S should be in writing. This is done in writing for two reasons: instructions given in writing with the C/S signing an acknowledgment that they have received the instructions will avoid any misunderstandings between the investigator and the C/S; and secondly the investigator will have the documents available for court purposes later if necessary. In the event that the actions of either the investigator or the C/S ever come into question at a later date, this documentation will be invaluable. The C/S should read and sign the registration paperwork in the presence of the investigator, who should check them for complete understanding of the registration and documentation process, and there should be another investigator present to act as a witness.

It is very common for potential C/Ss to balk at registering or signing any forms, usually based on their fear that their identity will somehow become known by virtue of their having signed the documents. A thorough explanation of the security associated with the entire process should dissuade their fears. The use of fictitious names and/or C/S numbers on receipt forms, for example, will demonstrate to the C/S the length to which the policy protects their identity. With regard to the C/S who will be paid for their services, it should be made very clear that without the proper documentation and administrative paperwork, there will be no payments.

C/S files should be initiated on every C/S who will be paid or compensated in any manner. The C/S who is not receiving payment, but who is providing services in order to mitigate criminal charges against them, should still be registered. In the event that the investigator is going to make any requests for leniency on behalf of the C/S this documentation will probably be required. Nowadays prosecutors are very leery of requesting leniency for anyone from a judge without some type of written documentation detailing what services the C/S has provided. Another reason for documenting even the services of the C/S who is not paid is so that if allegations of misconduct are ever leveled against the investigator, the documentation can be used to detail that this is a business relationship.

It is critically important that investigators keep in mind at all times that their C/Ss are usually involved to some extent in criminal activity and that they can never completely be trusted. This is a business relationship, similar to any business contract. When someone makes a major purchase or agrees to a service, a contract is signed so that all parties understand their obligations. What makes this situation any different? The department C/S policy must make certain that C/S files are maintained under very tight security with strictly controlled access. Access to the paperwork regarding C/Ss should obviously be strictly limited to those persons with the appropriate positions and need to know the information. A prison riot in New Mexico in 1980 illustrates the point: At the onset of the prison uprising, one of the first thing that rioting inmates went after were files relating to prisoners acting as C/Ss for the prison administration. The tortures that these inmates were subjected to were extremely heinous. Although nobody would have anticipated the fact that the inmates of the institution would ever forcibly gain access to these records, it did happen, with tragic results. Security over C/S files is something that investigators need to take very seriously, so that safeguards are in place that will serve to preclude the information from falling into the wrong hands. A comprehensive policy regarding use of C/Ss should include policy and paperwork relating to C/S registration, advisement of the C/S as to rules pertaining to them, permissible uses of official funds, payment policies, accounting for expended funds, and audits of the payment program.

C/S Registration

The registration of a C/S should include the following elements:

1. **Criminal history**–this needs to be a complete criminal history. In the event that allegations of misconduct are ever made regarding the C/S, the entire background of the C/S will come into question and should be known beforehand.
2. **Personal history**–to include family information, known associates, business interests, and employment history. In the event that the C/S must be located, this information may prove very beneficial.
3. **C/S registration documentation**–to detail the rules by which they are required to provide their services. (See the example provided in Appendix 14.)
4. **Complete debriefing reports**–the results of the initial debriefing interview must be documented.
5. **Fingerprints**–useful for identification purposes should the need arise.
6. **Photograph**–useful for identification purposes or for distribution to investigators involved in tactical operations in which the C/S is involved.
7. **Assignment of a fictitious name and C/S number**–to be used for receipts and reports
8. **Signature card**–used when the C/S is registered, so that a record exists of the signature of the actual name and any fictitious name(s) used by the C/S. This is a part of the C/S Registration card. The reason for the signature card is to be able to conclusively determine if in fact the C/S did sign for payments received. Allegations of investigators keeping funds that were allegedly paid are routine, and without the signature card on file to compare the C/S signature it is more difficult to refute these allegations.

This may seem like a great deal of information to gather and a great deal of extra work for the investigator, but strict adherence to these regulations may save headaches and embarrassment later. Insisting on adherence to the department's C/S policy will demonstrate to the investigator the importance of all elements of the program. There is a very straightforward model C/S registration and payment policy that could be utilized by a department of almost any size. (See the example provided in Appendix 15.)

C/S Payment Program

It is critical that investigators are made aware of the fact that proper registration of any C/S is required before any payments can be made. With regard to actually paying any C/S for information or services rendered, several elements must be considered, and the payment program for C/Ss should include at a minimum the following:

1. **Signed and witnessed receipts for any and all payments made.** These receipts should be signed by the C/S receiving the funds, the investigator providing the funds, and witnessed by another investigator or officer. By doing so, the integrity of the process is safeguarded, and in the event that allegations of wrongdoing or misuse of official funds are ever leveled against the investigator, these signed and witnessed receipts will prove beneficial.

2. **Proper documentation for receipts and/or expenditures of funds.** The funds used to pay for information are public funds. They may be allocated to the police department as part of the budget process, or they may be somehow donated to the police department for the express purpose of being utilized for such purposes. Another source of these funds is seizure money, which has been recovered from criminal suspects and awarded to the department by the courts. Regardless of where this money comes from, it is public money, and it must be subject to strict accounting procedures. All expenditures, regardless of the amount involved, must be completely and thoroughly documented. This is not only needed to account for the expenditures if allegations of misconduct are made at some future date, but more important, it's being done because it is the most responsible and professional manner in which to handle such funds.

3. **Proper documentation of the reasons for expenditures.** It is not enough to document the fact that funds were utilized to pay a C/S; it is equally important that the reason for the payment(s) be documented. If the payment is being made for intelligence infor-

mation, a confidential report should be completed by the investigator documenting the information received. Reports must be completed if the payment is being made for any other reason as well. These payments may be for such activities as making a controlled purchase of drugs or contraband, providing information leading to an arrest or search warrant, or making an undercover introduction of an officer to a criminal suspect.

4. **Periodic audit reports.** Each investigator who handles any official funds must complete a periodic audit report. This can be done on a monthly basis, and must include the amount of funds received, the amount of funds expended, the cases or activities for which the expenditures were made (reports detailing specific reasons for expenditures already accompany payment receipts), and the balance of funds remaining on hand or that were redeposited into the official funds account. This process should not be any more difficult than balancing one's checkbook at the end of the month.

5. **Full-scale semi-annual audits of the entire C/S program.** The investigative manager has the responsibility to conduct a full-scale semi-annual audit on the entire C/S program. This audit will not only examine the accounting trail for the funds expended, but should also examine the documentation regarding the use of C/Ss by all investigators to make certain that appropriate policy was strictly adhered to throughout the audit period. Investigators must be taught that payments should never be made in advance, or without the proper documentation. The temptation to do so will occur, particularly if the relationship between the investigator and the C/S is a long-term relationship and a friendship has developed. The C/S who is low on funds can be very convincing, and can definitely play on the sympathy of even the most hardened investigator. An investigator, with every intention of obtaining the signed paperwork later, needs only to be burned once by a C/S for providing funds up front. The best way to avoid this problem is to make certain that it doesn't happen the first time by insisting that no payments will ever be made without the required documentation.

Investigators will soon learn that paying too much for information or services will make them look like a chump, and paying too little for information or services will make them appear cheap. Unfortunately, there is no payment schedule that can be used as a reference for determining the amount to pay a C/S for their services. The payments are instead made on somewhat of a sliding scale, and the amounts are determined by several factors to include the type of crime involved, the status or desirability of the offender, the amount of drugs/contraband recovered, the value of the C/S to the department, and so on. I have found that the easiest method for a new investigator or an investigator new to the field of working with a C/S is to simply ask an experienced investigator for advice on how much to pay for a certain type of information or service. Once this is done a few times, the investigator will be able to estimate their own payment schedule, subject to supervisory approval.

SPECIAL CIRCUMSTANCE CONFIDENTIAL SOURCES

There are some special circumstance C/Ss, whose use can lead to some very significant embarrassment for the police department if they are not handled properly. These special circumstance C/Ss include the juvenile C/S, the probationer/parolee who is acting as a C/S, or the drug/alcohol abuser or addict who is working as a C/S.

Use of Juveniles as C/Ss

This should be avoided if possible, as their use can lead to serious issues relating to liability. In the event that a juvenile C/S is injured while working with police, the department will be subject to extensive criticism for placing the juvenile in a position of danger. In the event that a department does decide that the benefits of utilizing a juvenile as a C/S outweighs the inherent risk, they should only do so with the written authorization of the juvenile's parent or guardian.

Use of Parolees/Probationers as C/Ss

This practice also has some inherent problems. Part of the probation or parole agreement that is signed by the defendant as a condition of probation or parole is that they will avoid contact with criminals. By utilizing the probationer or parolee as a C/S, the investigator is asking them to have direct contact with criminals, thereby clearly violating the conditions of their parole or probation. The best method to utilize these individuals as C/Ss is to first contact their probation or parole officer and seek their approval to utilize them. This is advisable because first of all, it is a matter of professional courtesy to a fellow law enforcement officer to do so. It is also beneficial in that the probation or parole officer has a great deal of information regarding their clients, which may prove beneficial to the investigator. It might be worth knowing that the potential C/S is a pathological liar who can't be trusted. Should the investigator learn this through experience, or be spared the lesson by a cooperative probation or parole officer? In my experience, the only time that I have had a probation or parole officer deny permission to have their client work as a C/S is because of the poor track record of the client. This probably saved me and my department a great deal of personal heartache and potential embarrassment.

Use of Drug/Alcohol Abusers/Addicts as C/Ss

This practice comes with its own set of potential problems. The investigator must keep in mind that these people are motivated by the drug/substance first and foremost, and therefore the investigator must exercise extreme caution in dealing with them. This can be particularly critical when undercover operations are conducted that involve the C/S. To have the C/S suddenly go off the deep end due to his or her drug/alcohol abuse or addiction could spell disaster if it occurs at a critical juncture in the undercover operation.

One of the biggest problems that I have observed in supervising investigators working with C/Ss is the situation in which the investigator tor becomes romantically involved with the C/S. This seems to be a particularly difficult situation with male investigators; however, this is not always the case. In a recent internal investigation by the Chicago Police Department, the subject of the investigation, a 32-year veteran tactical officer, was alleged to have kept to himself information that one of his C/Ss had regarding a murder so that his C/S, who had been charged with beating an elderly woman, could benefit from the information. He was also accused of failing to report that another (female) investigator had a romantic relationship with the same C/S. Sometimes the use of a female C/S to target a male subject or vice versa can lead to allegations of entrapment based on the alleged promise (implied or stated) of sexual favors from the C/S to the subject of the investigation for his engaging in criminal acts. The investigative manager must also be vigilant that the investigators under their command are not putting themselves into positions of becoming romantically involved with their C/Ss. The dynamics of how these romantic relationships begin is really quite simple. The C/S might be someone who is attempting to get consideration from prosecutors regarding pending criminal charges. The investigator, who is the person who will be providing the prosecutor with information regarding the level of cooperation of the C/S, can become the "knight in shining armor" to the C/S "damsel in distress" and bad things can happen. The same can occur if the motivation of the C/S is revenge or if the C/S falls into the category of cop freak or wannabe. Unfortunately, I have seen some marriages, families, and careers go right down the drain because of a romantic relationship between an investigator and a C/S.

CONFIDENTIAL SOURCE/OFFICER UNDERSTANDING AND WORKING RELATIONSHIP

The investigative manager needs to make it very clear to all investigative personnel that there are certain rules and expectations that will be strictly adhered to in all of their dealings with C/Ss. This will only be taken seriously by investigators if the investigative manager makes it very clear that no deviation from these expectations will be tolerated.

Most importantly, investigators need to know that *the relationship with the C/S must be on a strictly professional basis.* This must be a mandatory rule for any investigator to follow. It must be made perfectly clear to the investigator that the C/S is not their drinking buddy or someone with whom they should hang out. This is a business relationship, where one individual is performing a service for another individual for some type of compensation. The compensation in this case may be money or consideration on criminal charges, but it is a business relationship.

The investigator must also be cognizant of the fact that another important aspect of the relationship is that **the investigator must be in control at all times**. The street-smart C/S will constantly attempt to gain control over the relationship, and the investigator must be made aware of the fact that this is likely to occur. Oftentimes this control will have to be reestablished, particularly when dealing with C/Ss motivated by ego or perverse motivations. Although this can usually be accomplished in a nonthreatening manner, it must be done by whatever means possible. Investigators must know that the manner in which they treat their C/Ss will have a large impact on their reputation on the street, and can lead to situations in which potential C/Ss will actually seek them out to provide information based on their reputation. Investigators must know that they should avoid making promises to the C/S that they're not prepared to keep, because this will damage the working relationship as well as their reputation.

They must know to explain his or her role carefully to the C/S, not only at the time the C/S is registered, but at anytime in the relationship where they feel it is necessary to reestablish the role. They must caution the C/S to remain confidential. Although it sounds rather stupid to think that a C/S would in fact "front themselves off" by making their position as a C/S known, it does occasionally happen. When the ego of the C/S gets in the way, particularly for those motivated by revenge, they sometimes can't resist the urge to let the suspect know who turned them in, often with tragic consequences to the C/S.

The investigator must make certain that the C/S is clear on the consequences of a double-cross or committing criminal acts, and that the C/S is cautioned against setting up any activity until after they confer with the investigator. This is a very common problem, particularly when the C/S has been allowed to lose sight of who is in control of the relationship. It is rather unnerving to receive a call from a C/S who has set something up without the knowledge or authorization of the investigator. Oftentimes this is done out of the C/S's own initiative, which is admirable, but it does go against the idea of who is in control of the relationship. I have found that the easiest way to dissuade a C/S from making unauthorized plans for operations is to simply refuse to become involved in their planned activity. This will cause them embarrassment and may cost the investigator a case or an arrest, but it is sometimes necessary for this type of corrective action to occur so that the C/S learns that their setting up unauthorized activity will not be tolerated. The C/S also needs to be cautioned against setting up a cover story for an undercover officer until authorized to do so by the undercover officer. Unfortunately, I had to learn this one the hard way. I had a C/S who, at my direction, set up an introductory undercover meeting for me with a well-known "fence," whose business consisted of purchasing stolen property from burglars. Immediately prior to our arrival at the suspect's business, the C/S casually mentioned that he'd already told the subject that he and I had met while doing time in the state prison. As soon as I met the fence, he began quizzing me about my "background," focusing on the time that I had supposedly done in prison. Fortunately for me, I had completed a college internship at the state prison in question, so I could carry on the conversation (I thought) pretty well. Unfortunately for me, he knew more than I did about the place and the meeting ended when he looked at me and said, "Nice try officer, now get the hell out of my place." I rather sheepishly left the premises, with both the C/S and I having learned a very valuable lesson.

Investigators must keep in mind that their C/Ss are usually criminals to begin with, and they must be cautioned against setting patterns with their meetings with a C/S. As mentioned earlier, for the most part these people were criminals before they agreed to work with the police and it is likely that they'll probably return to being a criminal when they're done. **They can never be completely trusted**.

Throughout the working relationship, investigators must avoid disclosing their operations and provide the C/S with **only what they need to know and nothing more**. They should avoid introductions of nonessential police personnel. They must check their C/Ss routinely for reliability by use of surveillance, undercover personnel, or feeding them information and seeing where it goes.

Although it seems very obvious, investigators must be cautioned against bringing the C/S to the police facility unless it is absolutely necessary. Most investigators have personal effects such as photos of their family, phone numbers and addresses of fellow officers, and confidential police reports in or near their work area. None of this should be in open view for a C/S to observe.

While mentioning this caution in a class I was teaching in Florida, an investigative commander from a Florida agency told the story of one of his subordinates who brought a C/S to the facility. The C/S was allowed to go unaccompanied to the restroom. A few weeks later the same C/S was arrested for impersonating a police officer, and recovered from his pocket was the badge of an officer who was killed in the line of duty and whose badge had been hanging on a plaque in the hallway near the restroom. This commander explained how embarrassing it was when the news media aired the story and the widow of the slain officer became aware of the situation.

The investigator must be made aware of the fact that he or she is responsible for the safety of the C/S, which is why both the initial contact and the relationship maintained with the C/S are critical. They have a professional as well as a moral obligation to their C/Ss, some of whom literally put their lives on the line to obtain information. Investigators should treat C/Ss like human beings, but must use caution and common sense when dealing with them. In most cases they need to be truthful, unless doing so would jeopardize ongoing police operations.

Investigators need to know that when dealing with a C/S "there is no such thing as a free lunch," and that they must be prepared to reciprocate for any favors performed by the C/S. They should expect calls at all hours for favors or to be informed of the latest "crisis" in the life of the C/S. The life of a C/S can get very lonely, and they may feel that the Investigator is their only "friend". Maintaining a friendly demeanor with a C/S is not a problem, but the Investigator can never lose sight of the fact that the first responsibility is to maintain a professional business relationship.

In the event that a C/S gets into trouble, the Investigator should be prepared to be called to testify on their behalf as a "character witness" to detail the cooperative efforts of the C/S with the police. If this occurs, the Investigator should expect some "heat" from the prosecutor's office in that they are now a "defense witness". This has happened to me on two occasions, and on both occasions the prosecutor was not at all happy to have a police officer on the stand making statements that were beneficial to the person that they were prosecuting.

It is my belief, however, that the Investigator has a "moral obligation" to the C/S. If the C/S has provided information that was used successfully against other criminals, that information should be made known to prosecutors if the C/S is in legal trouble, not in an effort to excuse their criminal behavior, but simply to make it known to prosecutors. There is a likelihood that the Investigator will not be viewed too favorably for doing so, but I feel that the damage to one's reputation and the abandonment of the moral obligation to the C/S necessitates this risk.

USING C/S INFORMATION IN SECURING SEARCH OR ARREST WARRANTS

Investigators must be aware that in the event that a search/arrest warrant is based upon C/S information, the credibility/reliability of the C/S must be established to the satisfaction of the judge issuing the warrant. This is another reason for the necessity of keeping documentation on C/Ss, as the information contained therein will be necessary to establish the credibility/reliability of the C/S.

Typically, when an Investigator utilizes information provided by a C/S in an application for a Search or Arrest Warrant, the following questions must be addressed:

1. How long has the Investigator known the C/S
2. How many times has this C/S provided information
3. What was the information about
4. How often was it acted upon
5. How many times did it result in arrests
6. How many times did it result in recoveries
7. How many of these cases resulted in convictions
8. How many of these cases are still pending
9. How does the C/S know that contraband/drugs exist in a certain place
   a. was he/she there?
   b. did he/she see it?
   c. how did he/she know what the substance or item was?
   d. is there more there?

Independent Corroboration of C/S Information

Investigators must be taught that regardless of the reliability of the C/S, there must be some *independent corroboration* of the information provided. If this independent corroboration is not provided, then the entirety of the Probable Cause for the issuance of the warrant rests solely on the information provided by the C/S. If this is the case, there is a much greater likelihood that the motion of the defendant to produce the C/S in court and to force the C/S to testify will be successful.

There are several methods for the Investigator to independently corroborate the information provided by the C/S, and they include:

1. Surveillance of the location
2. Researching the past criminal record of the subject
3. Independent verification of the occupants of the location/ residence

Unfortunately, some Investigators prefer to "take the easy way out", and base their applications for search or arrest warrants solely on the C/S information, usually due to the reliability of the C/S. Investigative Managers should insist that all C/S information be independently corroborated whenever possible, not only to lessen the chances of C/S disclosure in court, but to impress upon Investigators that the "easy way" is not always the "right way".

LEGAL CONSIDERATIONS FOR C/S UTILIZATION

There are important legal considerations that an Investigator must keep in mind when operating with a C/S. It is critical that the Investigator understands that the actions a C/S takes while under their supervision are in the capacity of an "agent" of the police. This means that they are bound by the same regulations regarding search & seizure as are the police. Illegal entries are just as illegal, illegal trespasses are just as illegal. The first legal consideration involves Entrapment, and the second consideration involved Disclosure.

Entrapment

Perhaps one of the most violated but also very avoidable legal issues that arises out the utilization of a C/S by an Investigator is the issue of entrapment. *Entrapment occurs if the conduct of the investigating officers or their agent (read C/S here) in dealing with the defendant would "likely" have induced a "normally law-abiding person" to commit the crime with which the defendant was charged.*

This issue is among the most hazardous aspects of working with a C/S for the detrimental impact that it can have on criminal cases. Entrapment needs to be seriously considered by Investigative Managers, and taught properly to Investigators.

Entrapment is a complete defense to a crime, which means a defendant is entitled to an acquittal if he committed the crime under circumstances constituting police entrapment. It does not matter that the evidence against the defendant was overwhelming. It does not matter that his guilt was undisputed. If he was entrapped, he goes free, it's just that simple.

Entrapment is what is known as an "affirmative defense," in that in order to claim entrapment, the defendant must first admit to having committed the crime. This might seem rather dangerous, and in fact it is, for if the entrapment defense doesn't work, the defendant is in a rather precarious position, already having admitted to the commission of the crime.

The issue of entrapment is regularly alleged in narcotics cases, often when undercover Officers are utilized, and almost always when a C/S is used. Many Judges with whom I have discussed the issue view entrapment as a type of lawless law enforcement, and a poor substitute for good solid investigative efforts. Utilizing entrapment to capture the bad guys is sometimes rationalized under the theory that "the end, when dealing with known criminals or the criminal classes, justifies the employment of illegal means."

I have a personal problem with this manner of thinking. If we can arbitrarily use whatever means we choose, including illegal means, to catch the bad guys, in my opinion the difference between us and them gets very blurry. The main issue with regard to entrapment comes down to the defendant's predisposition to commit the crime. Was the defendant predisposed to commit the crime, or was the defendant a "normally law-abiding person," who was induced to commit the crime by the conduct of the investigating officers or their agents?

C/S Disclosure

In addition to Entrapment, the second legal consideration involves Disclosure, which is when the court orders that the identity of the C/S be revealed or disclosed in court. This disclosure can take two forms, in the first form the Judge alone calls for the C/S to be brought before him or her in chambers to be interviewed, similar to securing a "John Doe" search warrant in which the C/S is interviewed by the Judge to determine Probable Cause. In the second (and far more destructive) form, the C/S is ordered to actually testify in open court, subject of course to cross-examination.

There are three main instances in which an C/S's disclosure can be ordered:

1. **If the probable cause for the arrest/search is based solely on the information provided by the C/S.** This is a very good reason for insisting that Investigators to independently corroborate information provided by a C/S
2. **When the C/S is a material witness to the offense,** which is a very good reason for Investigators to take steps to see to it that their C/Ss are as far away from actual criminal acts as possible.
3. **When the C/S is somehow "transactional" to the offense being charged,** such as setting up specifics of undercover purchases immediately before they take place. This is a relatively new concept, which seems to be gaining momentum among defense attorneys. Some prosecutors consider the C/S to be "transactional" to the offense if there has been any contact between the C/S and the defendant during a time period immediate prior to the offense taking place. As an example, in many cases an arbitrary time period such as 48 hours is set, and if any contact between the C/S and the defendant takes place within that period the C/S is considered "transactional" and disclosure is required.

Investigators should be made clearly aware of the issue of disclosure and take appropriate steps to avoid it. They should also school their C/Ss in the concept, and take precautions to avoid it. The biggest "selling point" when schooling the C/S in avoiding these disclosure situations is to explain that these precautions are for their own safety and well-being and to avoid their being placed on the witness stand.

If and when disclosure is ordered, Investigators must be cautioned against hiding the whereabouts of a C/S from the court. If disclosure is ordered, it is the responsibility of the Prosecutor to argue the order, and if they are unsuccessful the Investigator has no choice but to produce the C/S. I am aware of several situations in which Investigators have been "called to task" and chastised by Judges who thought that they were being less than truthful in their claims that they did not know the whereabouts of the C/S. I know of one narcotics Investigator who spent the evening in jail because of his refusal to identify the C/S, and have myself been ordered by a Judge to either reveal the identity of a C/S or request that the Prosecutor drop the charges.

C/S Dismissal

In the event that a C/S becomes problematic, too difficult to control, or intentionally engages in criminal conduct it may be better to dismiss them as a C/S and cease working with them. This is a difficult situation for the Investigative Manager, in that oftentimes Investigators are very reluctant to do so, citing the value of the C/S for current or future investigations. In these cases it must be pointed out to the Investigator that the C/S has become a "liability" and the potentially negative impact of continuing to work with the particular C/S outweigh the value of the continuing the relationship. Of course, this is often much easier said than done. In extreme cases, the Investigator may have to be actually ordered (verbally, in writing, or both) to cease working with a particular C/S.

Chapter 11

SUPERVISION OF UNDERCOVER PERSONNEL AND RAID AND ARREST PLANNING

There is no question that among the most challenging of supervisory duties is supervising undercover personnel and raid and arrest planning. The investigative manager who is responsible for supervision of an undercover officer (UC) is placed in an extremely high stress and demanding position. Having supervised and managed undercover officers in a variety of units, I can personally attest to the stress levels generated. It was always in the back of my own mind that, if anything happened to one of our UC officers or those officers conducting support duties such as surveillance, it would be my responsibility to inform their family members of their injury or death. That responsibility weighs very heavy in the mind of any law enforcement official, very similar to the responsibility of a commanding officer in the military who is responsible for sending soldiers into combat situations.

PURPOSES FOR UNDERCOVER OPERATIONS

There is no question that undercover work is inherently dangerous. Every time an investigator is sent out to work in an undercover capacity their lives are literally at risk. The investigative manager must be fully cognizant of this fact and appreciate the dangers that are inherent. It is the responsibility of the investigative manager to not only carefully plan undercover operations, but also to see to it that the UC officer understands his or her role and the necessary limitations to that role. Unplanned undercover operations are just as potentially danger-ous as are undisciplined undercover officers. In order to be effective and safe, a great deal of discipline is necessary, both on the part of the UC officer as well as on the part of the supervisor. Without this disci-pline, the already inherent danger of UC work is multiplied dramati-cally. The first step in establishing that discipline is to understand the purposes for undercover operations. They include:

- **Determine if a crime is being planned or committed.** Rather than working with a confidential source (C/S) whose reliability must first be established, a UC officer "inserted" into the crimi-nal's inner circle makes the question of credibility or accuracy of the observations a moot point.
- **Identify criminal associates and all persons involved.** This can preclude numerous hours of surveillance and possibly record searches. If a UC officer can be "inserted" into the criminal's inner circle, he or she can quickly observe and probably identify crimi-nal associates.
- **Obtain evidence for court.** Again, the issue of credibility is raised. If the UC officer obtains the evidence, they have assumed credibility over information provided by a C/S.
- **Locate contraband and/or stolen property.** Rather than depending on information provided by a confidential source, the UC officer, if given access to locations frequented by the suspect, can observe and identify contraband and/or stolen property.
- **Determine the most opportune time for a raid or arrest.** This is a particularly critical purpose. Conducting raids and making arrests is very dangerous work, and the more information that offi-cers conducting raids and arrests have prior to the operation the better. Information gathered by a C/S *may be accurate.* On the other hand, information gathered by a UC officer *will be accurate,* based on the UC officer's concern for the well-being of their fel-low officers.
- **Obtain information for search warrants.** Again, the issue of credibility is raised. If the UC officer obtains the evidence, they have assumed credibility over information provided by a C/S.
- **Test reliability of informants or witnesses.** In the event that investigators suspect the reliability of a C/S or the veracity of a

witness, sometimes an undercover operation can either substantiate or refute their suspicions.

QUALIFICATIONS FOR THE UC OFFICER

The nature of undercover work is that a great deal of autonomy is necessary for the undercover officer to function. In addition, initiative and creativity are not only very desirable traits for UC officers; they are in fact an integral part of their duties. However, this need for autonomy or the initiative and creativity of the UC officer are not such important components of the assignment that they preclude the need for careful planning and discipline. Unfortunately, problems often arise when the UC officer extends the boundaries of initiative and creativity, and engages in excessive or undisciplined creativity and initiative. Undercover personnel are at the absolute center of attention during the undercover operations, which can be rather intoxicating. This is especially true for the newer investigator, who is often selected for undercover assignments due to either their youthful appearance or for the fact that they are less likely to be recognized by criminals in the particular jurisdiction. As you can see, a UC officer must be level-headed. With this in mind, consider the following characteristics as good qualifications:

- **Self confidence.** Occasionally, I have seen the self-confidence of a UC officer border on egomania, but it is essential that the UC officer has complete confidence in his or her ability to complete the assignment safely.
- **Good judgment.** Undercover operations are no place for the insertion of an officer who continually displays questionable judgment. Making the right decisions, often under stressful and/or dangerous circumstances, is an essential element of a successful undercover operation.
- **Mental alertness.** While in an undercover capacity, the UC officer must be attuned to the slightest change in the suspect's demeanor, the arrival or involvement of unplanned accomplices, and many other issues that can act as danger signals. In addition, the UC officer must be able to remember minute details of inter-

actions during undercover operations and be able to document them later in investigative reports.

- **Resourcefulness.** As with much investigative work, things rarely go exactly according to plan. UC officers must have the ability to think on their feet during these circumstances and adjust their approach to the situation. The need for the UC officer to be resourceful can mean the difference between an operation going smoothly or ending in failure and possibly even disaster.
- **The UC officer must actually *want* to do it.** This is perhaps the most important qualification. Officers assigned to undercover work against their will are seldom if ever successful. Officers being assigned to UC work must clearly understand the inherent dangers and the potential for failure. They must be willing to put themselves in dangerous situations, relying on their own abilities and the abilities of their surveillance and backup officers to ensure their safety.

I can recall a situation when assigned as commander of a multi-agency Narcotics Task Force in which a young officer was assigned to the unit. This young man had all of the characteristics that should have made him an excellent UC officer. He was street-smart, well-versed in terminology and information regarding drugs, and did not present a threatening appearance in any way. After the first few assignments in which he was to participate in UC meetings with suspects however, it became apparent that something was very wrong. He was extremely concerned with the location of his surveillance units, and displayed so much nervous behavior with the suspects that they became nervous and ultimately told him that they weren't going to do business with him. After approximately a month in the Task Force, the officer approached me privately and asked that he be returned to his parent agency. When asked why, he readily admitted that although he wasn't leery of performing his patrol duties in uniform, he was terrified of going undercover, a fact that he didn't think to share with his own chief of police prior to being assigned to the Task Force. Needless to say, he was returned.

UNDERCOVER PREPARATION

Undercover operations require extreme preparation. No competent investigator would sit down to interview the key suspect in a homicide investigation without doing his or her homework, and neither should he or she ever be permitted conduct any undercover operations without doing his or her homework. Preparation for UC operations can mean the difference between a well-planned, successful operation and a disaster. Prior to initiating any UC operation, several actions should be completed:

1. As much information as possible should be gathered on the suspect and his associates.
2. Any planned or secondary meet spots and neighborhoods should be checked out ahead of time, both for familiarization with the area as well as to look for areas of potential danger.
3. The UC officer and the C/S (if used) should be quizzed on the cover story that they are using, and should anticipate questions that might be asked so as to have their answers ready.

It is imperative that UC officers never be permitted to attempt or conduct undercover operations without adequate surveillance. And they should always assume that the suspect will utilize countersurveillance. The UC officer must always remember that they are dealing with someone who admires deceit, dishonesty, and a good double cross. The investigative manager should never allow their UC personnel to underestimate the targets of the investigation or their associates.

It is often necessary that the undercover officer call the shots when operating on the street, but in order to do that effectively and safely, a great deal of discipline is necessary. In the event that a UC officer demonstrates that he or she does not possess this discipline, he or she should not be permitted to conduct UC operations. It's just that simple. The investigative manager must also show this discipline. Some managers don't want to appear as if they are stifling their UC officers, nor do they want to appear to be overly cautious. This can and often does lead to the investigative manager allowing their UC personnel to take absolutely unnecessary risks.

Unfortunately, it is common for UC officers to sometimes get caught up in what narcotics officers refer to as "kilo fever." This occurs when the desire to make the case gets so intense that the UC officer makes bad decisions and takes unnecessary risks just to get the buy down or the case concluded. It is equally unfortunate that some nvestigative managers fall prey to this type of thinking. This can lead to very poor judgment on the part of the investigative manager, the very person who is ultimately responsible for not only the success of the operation, but also for the safety of their subordinates. Too many risks are taken, limits are stretched, and well-established boundaries are ignored, all in the name of getting the case done and catching the bad guy. Having been to hospital rooms and funerals of officers injured or killed in the line of duty, it has always been my opinion that there aren't any suspects or cases worth risking the life of an officer.

UNDERCOVER OPERATIONAL PLANNING

One method of minimizing the inherent dangers of UC operations while maximizing the safety of all participants is to insist on a written operational plan. There are several reasons for this.

- All personnel, regardless of experience level, know exactly what their responsibilities are.
- With a written plan, crucial elements of the raid/arrest are less likely to be overlooked.
- The discipline involved in formulating and writing an operational plan can assist in the training of investigative personnel.

The written operational plan necessitates that the writer demonstrate a logical sequence of events, that all elements of the plan are addressed in a complete manner, and that contingency planning for unforeseen changes is addressed. In addition, this plan requires an expository style of writing, in which extraneous information is omitted. The writer must simply stick with the facts. A written operational plan need not be elaborate, but at a minimum, it should include:

- Complete identifiers (if known) of offender(s)
- Vehicle descriptions
- Map of the area in which the operations are to take place, with photos if possible

- A thorough plan of action
- Specific assignments for all personnel
- Contingency planning for as many unforeseen circumstances as can be imagined.

The operational plan should be as simple and straightforward as possible, so that all participants in the operation will understand it clearly and be able to complete their assignments. (See the example provided in Appendix 16.) A plan must be discussed with the UC officer and sometimes even rehearsed prior to the operation. In addition, decisions must be made ahead of time as to how much latitude will be afforded the UC officer in any deviations from the plan. Examples of some issues you might need to work out include:

- How much discretion will the UC officer have when deciding whether or not to enter a building or vehicle with suspects?
- How many moves from the original meet location will be permitted?
- Will the suspect be permitted to enter the UC officer's vehicle?
- What happens if additional suspects show up unannounced?

The basic plan, however, must be *strictly* adhered to under any circumstances. It's much better to call off an operation than attend a funeral. In the event that a UC officer repeatedly demonstrates that he or she cannot operate according to the plan, he or she should not be allowed to work undercover.

RAID AND ARREST PLANNING

Unlike patrol assignments, where most arrests are on-view or unplanned, most arrests by investigative personnel allow for advanced planning. Investigators and investigative managers should take advantage of this opportunity and conduct careful planning for any raid or arrest. As with UC operations, insistence on a written plan can reduce some of the inherent danger in these operations. Much of the same information necessary for a raid or arrest plan will be contained in an operational plan, but additional information will be needed. This includes:

- A diagram of the location to be searched
- Potential locations of contraband, evidence, or suspects
- Whether children or other noninvolved persons are on the premises
- Specific information such as door swings, window placement, alarm systems, dogs on the premises
- I would recommend that the concept known as "Deconfliction" be seriously considered. Deconfliction means checking well ahead of time with other agencies to determine if any other agency might be targeting the offender(s). Oftentimes, particularly with well-known and very active offenders, several agencies might have investigations going on the same offenders at the same time. Needless to say, this could prove dangerous or even disastrous if more than one agency decides to make the raid or arrest while another agency is doing the same thing.
- While serving as the Commander of a large multi-agency drug enforcement task force we learned how important Deconfliction can be, almost the "hard way." We had been working a narcotics investigation on a very active subject for several months and had decided to conduct a search warrant execution on a particular day. Unbeknownst to us, the U.S. Drug Enforcement Adminstration (DEA) was working on the same subject and had planned a large undercover purchase on the same day of our planned raid. Fortunately for us, one of our personnel recognized some DEA vehicles and personnel down the street from our subject's business. We contacted them immediately and learned of their activity. Needless to say, we backed off on our plan and they continued with their investigation. I've often reflected on that incident, wondering what would have happened if we had conducted our raid while their undercover agents were on the premises.
- I hate going to police funerals, and to have been instrumental in causing one would have been truly tragic for all involved.
- Any other information that is needed.

When I began my law enforcement career, I was taught that the key to any successful raid/arrest is to follow the *"Six S"* plan:

- Superiority of manpower
- Superiority of firepower

• Simplicity
• Surprise
• Speed
• Safety.

The investigative manager must ensure that all six elements are part of the raid/arrest plan. There is, however, one more element common to both UC operations and raid/arrest planning. That is what I call the "X" factor. The "X" factor refers to the fact that no matter how well an operation is planned and no matter how well staffed an operation may be, there is always the possibility that things can go wrong. The investigative manager should always remember this "X" factor, and not get too self-assured that everything will go according to plan. At the last minute things can be thrown into the mix by the suspect, the UC officer, or some other source through no fault of anyone. You therefore need to plan for as many contingencies as possible, and constantly play the devil's advocate. By doing so, you can minimize the inherent danger and maximize the potential for a safe, successful operation.

Chapter 12

EVALUATING PERFORMANCE OF INVESTIGATIVE PERSONNEL

Evaluating investigators is different than evaluating patrol officers. Patrol officers engage in much more quantifiable activities, such as the number of citations written, abandoned cars processed, and so on. The activities of investigators rarely lend themselves to quantification, so there is no real scorecard to determine how well an investigation was conducted. An evaluation of an investigator is much more subjective. This not only makes the evaluation more difficult to do, but it also makes the completed evaluation more difficult to explain and defend.

COMMON ERRORS DURING EVALUATIONS

In many investigative units, performance evaluation time is a difficult period, full of mistrust and hurt feelings. This difficult time is often compounded by a number of common errors that supervisors make when putting together evaluations. First is the *error of common tendency*. This is where all personnel are evaluated toward the middle of the scoring scale in an effort to keep everyone on an even keel and avoid conflicts with subordinates. Managers who make this mistake fail to realize that, although they might make the moderate performer happy, they are infuriating the outstanding performers who feel that they have been somehow graded on a curve and that their excellent efforts were not recognized in the evaluator's attempt to not anger anyone. The poor performer, on the other hand, just got a gift of a moderate evaluation when their performance should have resulted in a much lower evaluation.

A second common error is the *halo effect*, in which the investigator who has performed at a poor or moderate level throughout the evaluation cycle suddenly performs some outstanding act. This might be an act of heroism, an exceptionally well-done investigation, or something else that stands out. This single incident is allowed to distort the entire evaluation, and the poor or moderate performer receives an unduly positive performance evaluation.

A third error is the *horns effect*, which is, as you might imagine, the opposite of the halo effect. This is where an investigator who has performed at an excellent level throughout the evaluation cycle suddenly commits some type of error or transgression. This might be an act of poor judgment, a poorly done investigation, or something else that stands out as a negative. This single incident is allowed to distort the entire evaluation, in this case leading to an unduly negative performance evaluation.

Perhaps the most common error when evaluating the performance of investigators is *using inconsistent evaluation standards*. Many agencies use the same evaluation format for investigators that they use for patrol officers. The problem is that the specific dimensions used on the evaluation form for patrol may not apply to the position or duties of investigators. Many organizations are beginning to address this issue by customizing the evaluation instruments used for investigators as well as for other positions within the department. This leads to consistency and ensures that the tasks actually associated with the various positions are the tasks being evaluated. We'll come back to that in a moment.

THE EVALUATION PROCESS

The heart of any evaluation is the process. That in itself is relatively simple, in that it only consists of four steps:

1. The subordinate is informed of expected behavior.
2. The subordinate is observed.
3. These observations are documented.
4. Managerial feedback is given to the subordinate.

In applying this process, there are dimensions or types of skills and abilities that are common to both patrol personnel and investigators. These include:

- Working under stress
- Interpersonal skills
- Legal knowledge
- Decision making
- Oral communications.

At the same time, you should consider certain dimensions from the investigative perspective, such as:

1. **Productivity.** As discussed earlier, this is easier to evaluate if you are dealing with quantifiable activities, such as patrol/traffic duties, instead of dealing with the nonquantifiable duties of an investigator. Productivity from the investigative standpoint refers to whether the investigator is capable of accomplishing work within a reasonable time and using available resources.
   - *Can the investigator plan tasks in a logical fashion and complete tasks on or ahead of schedule?*
2. **Initiative.** Due to the necessity for investigators to be somewhat autonomous and self-starting, this is a very important consideration.
   - *How much supervision does the investigator need?*
   - *Does the investigator demonstrate persistence in following steps to complete assignments?*
   - *Following the appropriate training and time in the assignment, can the investigator operate independently?*
3. **Written communication.** This is the lifeblood of the investigative unit. All investigators must be able to write clearly and accurately.
   - *Is the investigator's written work understood by readers?*
   - *Can the investigator comprehend written communications?*
4. **Investigative techniques.** The investigator must be able to recognize and document the elements of a crime.
   - *Can the investigator recognize M.O.s and collect pertinent evidence?*
   - *Can the investigator cultivate and utilize confidential sources effectively?*

- *Can the investigator effectively interview and interrogate people?*
- *How are the investigator's surveillance techniques?*

5. **Use of time.** This is a key element, given the autonomy that most investigators have.
   - *Does the investigator use time appropriately?*
   - *Does the investigator have difficulty handling the lack of structure that is part of the job?*

During performance evaluations, objectivity is paramount. You should base your evaluations on observations and documented information, not feelings. I have always been taught that the key to successful performance evaluations of any personnel consists of documenting both the good work and the not-so-good work. Keeping something as simple as a manila folder for each investigator and inserting notes and copies of both positive and negative documents throughout the evaluation cycle can not only lead to accurate and objective performance evaluation, but it can also provide you with documentation (and sometimes justification) if the evaluation is challenged. When a portion or the entire evaluation is challenged, the person making the challenge deserves to be provided with the facts that led to the evaluation scores. The employee doesn't care to hear about your opinions or feelings. They want and should be given documented details of the specific behaviors and/or shortcomings that led to the evaluation.

DESIGNING A CUSTOMIZED EVALUATION INSTRUMENT

As indicated earlier, many departments are starting to custom design their own evaluation instruments for various positions besides those related to patrol assignments. This might result in separate instruments for clerical, dispatch, and investigative assignments. These customized tools not only ensure that the performance of these personnel is being evaluated based on what they actually do, but they can boost morale because subordinates feel they are being treated more fairly. The positive effects of the entire experience can also have a long-term impact. This is due in large part to the agency administration showing enough interest in fair and objective performance evaluations that they are willing to expend the time and effort to design an evaluation instrument that more accurately evaluates investigative personnel. There are a number of other advantages as well:

- Gets employees involved in their own evaluation system
- People are more likely to meet standards that they help set
- Sets consistent standards for management
- Forces management to document facts instead of feelings
- Diminishes chances for exaggeration (positive or negative) by managers
- Forces management and labor to work together as a team to develop the process
- Can diminish grievances for substandard work, because the union helped set the standard
- Forces management to keep records of employee performance during the cycle.

Designing a custom performance evaluation instrument for investigators does not have to be an ordeal. In fact, it can be a team-building exercise. I have used the following process and was very pleased with the results of our efforts. The design process itself begins by assembling an evaluation instrument design committee. It is advisable to seek out volunteers first and have participants from all ranks. If your agency has a collective bargaining agreement, I recommend that the labor union be involved in the entire process.

Once the committee is established, the process can begin. Seating in the room should be arranged so that all participants feel free to express themselves openly. A U-shaped configuration helps all participants feel included, and eliminates rank or position as much as possible. (See the example provided in Appendix 17.) A laptop computer and an LCD projector should be installed in the center, with a keyboard person (who knows how to type) on hand and a screen on which to project the computer screen. The open end of the "U" should face the screen. Flip charts/blackboards should be available for brainstorming. Once the process begins and the participants realize they have the power to voice their opinions, there will be many ideas to be captured. The process of designing the instrument should be carefully explained to the participants, as should the overall goal: *To develop a fair, consistent, and objective evaluation instrument, based on the actual duties of the employees as compared to a consistent set of standards.*

Begin the process by discussing the current instrument in an effort to identify those dimensions that should be kept. In the event that no dimensions are to be kept, you'll have to start from scratch. One method of generating ideas is to make certain that all participants know that there are no stupid ideas or suggestions and that they should speak their mind throughout the process. You shouldn't worry about anyone being overly negative. Actually, any participant who complains excessively will usually be the subject of commentary from the other participants.

The first time I was involved in this process, the committee included a union official. This particular officer was known for his dislike of the agency's administration, the city government officials, and just about anyone else in a position of authority. At the onset of the process, all participants were encouraged to speak their minds, and this officer took the opportunity to begin ranting and raving about everything and everybody. After about five minutes, several of the other participants begin telling him to stick with the process and to save his complaints for people who actually wanted to hear them.

If you feel that the level of existing conflict will not allow the process to proceed in an orderly manner, have a facilitator present. The on-site manager can settle disagreements, which should be expected. There is nothing wrong with disagreement during the process, as long as the intent of the disagreements is to complete the desired goal. Disagreement and arguments can be healthy, as long as they don't get out of hand and become personal. They can also serve to identify existing conflicts that might need to be addressed later. If the arguments begin to repeat themselves, the on-site manager or facilitator can make the decision to move on to the next topic.

Groups can usually reach agreement on each dimension. As they do, the keyboard operator puts it on the computer screen for all participants to review. I have found that using a computer adds to both the spontaneity of the ideas presented as well as to the more rapid flow of the process. Trying to capture ideas on flip charts or blackboards works for a while, but when the ideas need to be modified and rewritten, the process can bog down and get messy. Using the computer and an LCD allows instant rewrites and corrections, which keeps the process moving along.

I strongly recommend continuing the process until you're done. If you quit and come back, you'll have to reestablish control. Not only will you have to start all over again, but the same arguments from the first process will arise again and will have to be addressed again.

As you can see, designing customized evaluation instruments involves additional work, but it's well worth the effort. I believe that all employees want is a fair shake. This process does that. At the very least, it gives them a say in the instrument used to evaluate them, the backbone of the entire evaluation process.

Chapter 13

MANAGING MARGINAL PERFORMERS

Police departments spend thousands of dollars recruiting, testing, screening, and training prospective police officers. In addition, we spend months providing field training officer programs to our new personnel. With regard to investigators, we take this several steps further. We carefully screen, select, and train them to increase their chances for success. And yet, with all of this hard work and expense, we still seem to have some investigative personnel who just don't get it. If we don't come up with a strategy to not only *deal with* them, but actually *address* the issue, we will continue to live with not only their lack of activity but also with the myriad of additional problems that these people cause within the investigative unit.

WHAT IS A MARGINAL PERFORMER?

No matter how hard we try, some personnel never seem to rise above the level of barely making it. I refer to these personnel as marginal performers, who consistently seem to do just barely enough to get by. There are several definitions of a marginal performance, but I feel that the most succinct is the following: *A marginal performing employee is one who is aware of standards and expectations and yet repeatedly fails to meet those standards and expectations.*

In the final analysis, marginal/poor performance is whatever the supervisor deems it to be, and it can vary from employee to employee completing the same task. Nobody would expect the new investigator to perform as well as the seasoned veteran. If Michael Jordan, during the peak of his career, scored 15 points during an NBA game it would have been considered a dismal performance. An NBA rookie playing in his first game, on the other hand, scoring the same 15 points would probably be seen as a superstar. Similar to evaluation of overall performance, determining marginal/poor performance is more difficult in job assignments that are not easily quantifiable, such as in investigative assignments. You need to consider all aspects of the job. Don't just look at the most obvious, such as good/bad performance on a particular assignment. This is somewhat similar to the halo or horns effect in evaluations.

Recognizing marginal/poor performance is often made more difficult when you have a personal relationship with the employee. This is particularly true in smaller agencies, in which officers have grown up on the job together and have known each other for a long time. It is sometimes very difficult to separate the friendship from the performance. Supervisors commonly defend their friend's performance when it is questioned, rather than to admit to a critic (or to themselves) that their friend's performance is not adequate.

A rather common pitfall occurs when the investigative manager accepts comments or performance evaluations from past supervisors to determine the usual level of performance of an investigator. You never really know how much objectivity went into those comments or evaluations. Personal observation, rather than a review of someone else's feelings and/or observations, is much more valuable when determining an investigator's level of performance.

UNDERSTANDING LEVELS OF PERFORMANCE

A number of years ago I was on a flight to somewhere to present a class to a group of police officers. To while away the time I began to read the "in-flight" magazine and came across an article on management. In the article it stated that employees usually fall into one of three categories: Very Good, Very Bad, or Acceptable. The article didn't address what percentages were in these categories.

As I read that article it struck me that although this was true, it was my experience that the problem for managers was not determining which subordinates fell into these categories, the problem was what to do about the employees in the middle "acceptable" category. It has been my experience that there are only about 10% of subordinates that fall into the "very bad" category—let's call them "defective." There are also about 10% of subordinates that fall into the "very good" category-let's call them "effective." That leaves 80% in the middle—let's call them "reflective."

The "effective" personnel show up every day, ready to go to work. They excel at every task assigned to them, seem to thrive under pressure, are constantly looking for new and/or better ways to do things, and are truly a blessing for their managers.

The "defective" personnel are the type whose pulse you feel the need to check every morning just to make sure that they are still alive. They seem to always find the "easy way" to perform a task, spend more time looking for ways to get out of work than they would getting it done, and are responsible for taking up an inordinate amount of a manager's time. These are often the employees who constantly complain about anything and everything, and who can find fault in their coworkers, the agency, the government, and everything else. They often devote their energy to things like associations which attempt to set the work conditions and requirements that they themselves don't actually meet anyway.

The "reflective" personnel show up every day, do what is asked of them, and we really don't have to spend much of our time with them. The reason why I call them "reflective" is because that is exactly what they are doing on a daily basis. They are going about their business and constantly "reflecting" on two things:

1. How are the top 10% "effective" personnel being rewarded and recognized by management for their exceptional contributions?
2. What is management doing to address the laziness and lack of contribution of the bottom 10% "defective" personnel?

If these folks come to the conclusion that the "effective" personnel are not being properly rewarded or recognized for their exceptional contributions, then why should they strive to be like them? If they come to the conclusion that nothing is being done to address the lack of effort of the "defective" personnel, why not gravitate toward them? You've got to admit, it is much easier to come to work and not do much than it is to come to work and excel. Taking personal pride out of the equation, if it's easier to do the bare minimum and expend as little effort as possible, why not do so?

Managers that are not recognizing the Investigators that constantly do an exceptional job or addressing the investigators that are not doing the job run the risk of driving these "reflective" personnel the wrong direction.

When determining the performance of an investigator, a simple equation comes to mind, regardless of rank or assignment:

Performance = Ability x Support x Effort

This equation means that high levels of work performance result from the combination of a person's job-related abilities, various forms of organizational support, and individual work efforts. If an employee's performance falls short of expectations, you can use the equation to help identify the reasons why. The first factor to consider is ability. The screening process is supposed to determine whether a prospective employee possesses the basic abilities, but the screening process is not infallible, even when considering all of the money and time spent on psychological exams, polygraphs, medical exams, and background investigations. In addition to possessing these abilities, individuals must *believe* in their personal abilities if they are to perform well. Police academies spend a great deal of time trying to instill in new officers this personal belief and confidence, but it shouldn't stop there. Supervisors and managers have a responsibility to help build and maintain self-confidence and to help the employee realize that he or she can meet high-performance expectations. In my opinion, the two greatest fighting forces in the world are the United States Marine Corps and the Foreign Legion. Part of the reason for the incredible successes and legendary heroism of these two organizations is that their members are trained to actually *believe* that they are as good as they say they are.

Support refers to support from management. Even the most hard-working and capable individuals will be unable to maximize their performance if they do not have the necessary support from management. This support includes the physical as well as the social aspects of the job, which should be maximized by the supervisor. An investigator who is having a tough time getting reports in on time or in an acceptable condition might benefit from spending a few hours a week (on department time) working on a tutorial for a word-processing computer program.

Effort refers to the amount of energy (physical or mental) that a person applies to perform a task. Capable, well-supported but uninspired employees are no more likely to succeed than hard-working persons who lack the ability or the support. The difficulty with effort, however, is that the decision to exert or withhold effort can only be controlled by the individual.

After determining that an investigator is performing at a marginal or poor level, you must first determine if the employee has always been a marginal/poor performer or if this undesirable performance has been a recent change. If you see this deteriorating job performance in an otherwise capable and effective employee, there could be some underlying factors at work. It may be due to illness (either personal or family), marital or relationship problems, alcohol or drug abuse issues, problems with children or coworkers, or a variety of other personal problems. It may be due to the effects of stress, which can be the result of personal or work conflicts. Don't ignore the possibility of posttraumatic stress, which can manifest itself long after the stress-inducing situation or incident has passed. In many cases, this posttraumatic stress may not even related to what most people would consider a life-threatening situation or incident; it may be something that the individual *perceived* as being extremely stressful.

HOW TO ADDRESS THE MARGINAL PERFORMER

Regardless of the reasons, you must take action after identifying a marginal or poor-performing investigator. What follows is a 9-step process for doing that:

1. **Make certain that the desired performance standards are known and understood.** If you require that investigative reports be submitted no longer than 48 hours after the activity is completed, this should be communicated to your personnel. Persons can only be held responsible for what they know is expected.
2. **Bring the performance deficiency to the individual's attention ASAP.** Rather than wait for the evaluation cycle to end in a

formal evaluation, you should inform the individual as soon as possible that his or her performance is not up to the expected standard. Using the report-writing example, explain the 48-hour rule for report submission again and then show the individual that he or she has repeatedly failed to comply.

3. **Ask in a nonthreatening manner for an explanation of the substandard performance.** Perhaps the substandard performance is based on a current illness in the family or some other personal issue, or perhaps the investigator has no plausible explanation at all.

4. **Describe the implications of the substandard work, but do so in a nonthreatening manner.** Rather than telling the employee what you're going to do to him or her, I would suggest telling the employee what he or she is doing to himself or herself or what he or she is *forcing* you to do.

5. **Restate the original (and still desirable) performance objectives.** Do this clearly and understandably. Ask the officer to repeat the objectives to you. Use their own feedback to determine their understanding of the expectations.

6. **Offer the external support necessary for the marginal/poor performer to improve his or her performance.** Using our report-writing example, perhaps allowing the investigator to learn to use or improve his or her use of a word-processing program may address the issue.

7. **Express confidence that the marginal/poor performer will respond as expected.** I don't believe an investigator's performance can be improved by constantly belittling them. When you express confidence in an investigator's talent, that investigator often rises to the level of the confidence you expressed.

8. **Agree on an appropriate timeframe for jointly evaluating the investigator's improvement.** Don't make this timeframe too far away or he or she may forget what it was you discussed in the first place. And don't make it too soon or he or she may feel like you're breathing down his or her neck. Of course, when discussing the follow-up meeting, the marginal/poor performer will undoubtedly claim that he or she will meet (and probably exceed) your stated expectations by the next meeting. Don't allow the person to fail by expecting him or her to meet all your performance standards at once. Develop an incremental plan for meeting the

stated objectives. Set an agreed-upon goal that he or she is more likely to achieve by the next meeting. If the individual can achieve this goal, the fact that he or she did so successfully will possibly instill enough self-confidence to succeed in achieving your expectations in time.

9. **Keep in mind that few employees are terminal marginal/ poor performers.** However, if none of the previous steps generate better performance, you will have to take additional steps. For this reason, the activities of investigators who don't show a turnaround must be closely monitored and documented.

Ultimately, addressing the issue of the marginal/poor investigator will come down to determining whether he or she should remain in his or her current assignment, be transferred to another investigative assignment, or be returned to patrol. When an investigator repeatedly demonstrates that he or she cannot meet minimum, reasonable performance standards, sending them back to patrol might not be the best choice for the agency. This issue becomes particularly difficult in agencies that have a permanent rank or position of investigator. The fact that this is a permanent rank can sometimes preclude the department from transferring the marginal/poor performer out of an investigative assignment.

There is an alternative course of action. The marginal/poor performer can be the subject of progressive disciplinary action. If it is determined that this is the most desirable course of action, you must carefully document all of the substandard performance during the investigative assignment. This documentation must be accurate, timely, and must record observations rather than feelings. Typically, an investigator subject to progressive disciplinary action for poor performance has been around long enough to fight the disciplinary action through some sort of an appeal. In order to defend the decision to initiate disciplinary action, you must be able to answer some of the following questions that are likely to arise during an appeal:

• Were your expectations clearly made known to the employee?
• Did the employee receive the same training as coworkers?
• Did the employee receive timely notification of their performance deficiencies?
• Did the employee have a reasonable time in which to improve his or her performance to an acceptable level?

Clearly stated and objective expectations, along with performance documentation, are the keys to successful supervision and management. Performance documentation is also one of the keys to successfully defending yourself against legal challenges following disciplinary action. Whether you use a computer program or a manila folder, keeping accurate and objective data on investigator performance is a critical element of managing the investigative unit.

The good new is the number of investigators who can be considered marginal performers is extremely small. From that number, the number of investigators whom you ultimately have to transfer or dismiss is even smaller. When you have clear, measurable requirements for investigative positions and you use a stringent selection process, you usually end up with the cream of the crop from patrol.

CONCLUSION

It is my heartfelt belief that the job of the investigative manager is among the most critical and most rewarding in the law enforcement profession. Investigators and investigative units that are properly and competently managed can do some really great things. On the other hand, units and investigators that are not properly or competently managed can cause some incredible damage, both to their agencies and to our profession. I sincerely hope that some of the material in this book will provide some ideas, techniques, and strategies to assist you in competently and professionally managing your own investigative unit.

Teaching all over the world allows me to meet a great number of cops. Many of these are investigators and/or investigative managers, and I have always been impressed with their desire to learn and improve. I have also been impressed with their dedication to our profession and to their assignments and duties. I am very appreciative of what they have taught me. I have learned something valuable from each class I have conducted. I have also walked away having made some new friends, for which I am very grateful. I always end my classes with an overhead slide that contains what is my basic philosophy toward our profession.

We should never forget that those of us privileged enough to be in the law enforcement profession are truly doing God's work:

- *We get the privilege of protecting those who need protection.*
- *We get the privilege of standing up for what is right and good in society.*
- *We occasionally get the privilege to right some of life's wrongs.*

DISCUSSION QUESTIONS

Chapter 1

1. How can the newly assigned investigative manager with no investigative background overcome this obstacle and develop credibility with their subordinates?

Chapter 2

1. What are some of the benefits of intelligence gathering that apply to the overall mission of the department?
2. Other than basic police academy training, what are some other methods available to ensure that patrol officers are able to conduct thorough preliminary investigations?
3. What are some benefits to utilizing case screening?

Chapter 3

1. Why is it essential to include patrol officers in the initial steps of the investigative process, and how do they benefit from this inclusion?
2. What methods might be used to move a department from the basic model of patrol involvement in the investigative process to an expanded role?

Chapter 4

1. What types of specialization of investigators would be necessary in your own department if staffing and budget permitted?

2. What steps could be taken to diminish the amount of the elitist mentality that specialists sometimes develop?
3. In the event that your agency needed more investigative personnel, how could you sell the idea to upper management and/or government officials?

Chapter 5

1. In the event your agency has permanent ranks for investigators, what are the positive benefits of having the permanent rank?
2. What types of justifications could be made for pay incentives for investigators, and how could these be justified to budget personnel?
3. What are some equitable methods for distributing call-out procedures for investigators?

Chapter 6

1. What would be the benefit of making patrol supervisors a part of the investigator selection process?
2. When considering the personnel records of applicants, what information should be viewed as the most indicative of potential success for the investigative applicant?
3. Compare your own agency's method of selection of investigative personnel with some of the strategies in this chapter and discuss how your own methods are either more effective or could be improved.

Chapter 7

1. What type of initial training does your agency provide for new investigators, and how might this be improved?
2. Besides the basic investigative training topics discussed in this chapter, are there any specific areas of training from which new investigators in your own agency might benefit?
3. How do you feel temporary or rotational assignments to your agency's investigative unit would be accepted? Would they benefit your agency?

Chapter 8

1. Why is it that some very effective patrol supervisors make very ineffective investigative supervisors? What could they do to improve their chances for success?
2. How could investigators be made more accountable without stifling their creativity or unduly restricting their freedom of movement and autonomy?
3. Is the span of control over investigative personnel adequate in your own agency? If not, how could the situation be improved?

Chapter 9

1. What type of case screening does your agency utilize, and is it effective? If not, how could the process be improved?
2. What steps could be taken in your own agency to ensure that case assignments and caseloads are as equitable as possible?
3. Is security over your agency's investigative data adequate? If not, how could security be improved?

Chapter 10

1. What are the most productive sources of Confidential Sources in your department?
2. How can an investigative manager reduce the possibility of inappropriate conduct by investigators utilizing Confidential Sources?
3. How much control should the investigative manager exert over the payment of Confidential Sources?

Chapter 11

1. When supervising investigators working in an undercover capacity, is it critical that the supervisors themselves have experience working undercover?
2. What steps could be taken to ensure that the undercover officer doesn't become so enmeshed in the undercover role as to begin making inappropriate decisions?

3. How could your own agency's raid and arrest planning be improved? Are there any items of specialized equipment or any specialized training that might benefit from your efforts?

Chapter 12

1. What are the differences between the evaluation instruments for patrol and investigative personnel in your agency? Are these instruments adequate, or is there a need for improvement?
2. Are there any specific evaluation dimensions on which investigators from your own agency need to evaluated?

Chapter 13

1. How are marginal performers addressed in your agency? Are there any mechanisms in place to attempt to motivate them, and if not, how could this issue be addressed in a manner that would be accepted by department administration and investigative personnel?
2. What types of reasons for marginal performance have you encountered, and how did you address the issues? What could you have done to improve how you handled these situations?
3. How do union contracts sometimes limit the ability of police managers to address the marginal performer, and how might these issues be improved?

APPENDICES

APPENDIX 1
INVESTIGATIVE RESPONSIBILITIES

POLICE DEPARTMENT GENERAL ORDER INVESTIGATIVE RESPONSIBILITIES

I. PURPOSE
To define and delegate investigative responsibilities to the operating divisions of the _____ Police Department in order to promote mutual cooperation and coordination, and to avoid duplication of effort within the department.

II. POLICY
It is the policy of the _____ Police Department to adopt procedures that will ensure the effective and efficient detection, apprehension, and prosecution of those persons who violate criminal laws.

III. DEFINITIONS
The following definitions are applicable to this order:

A. *Preliminary Investigation:* the activities undertaken by an officer(s) who responds to the scene of a crime, including:
1. providing aid to the injured
2. protecting the scene to ensure that evidence is not lost or contaminated
3. determining if an offense has actually been committed, and if so, the exact nature of the offense
4. determining the identity of the suspect or suspects, and the effect of an arrest if it can be accomplished at the scene or through immediate pursuit
5. furnishing other units, through the communications center, descriptions, method and direction of flight, and other relevant information regarding wanted persons or vehicles
6. obtaining complete identification of all witnesses
7. determining the need for investigative specialists and assistance
8. compiling a thorough and accurate report of activities.

B. *Follow-up Investigation:* an extension of the preliminary investigation. The purpose of the follow-up investigation is to provide additional investigation in order to effect the arrest of an offender and/or recover stolen property.

Basic activities of the follow-up investigation include:
1. identification and apprehension of the offender
2. arranging for the analysis and evaluation of evidence
3. recovery of stolen property
4. in-depth interviewing of victims and witnesses
5. interrogation of suspects
6. determining the involvement of the suspect in additional crimes
7. recording information obtained
8. preparation of the case for court presentation.

C. *Major Offense:* a real or suspected crime of such severity that it creates, or seems likely to create, an intense public demand for identification, apprehension, and prosecution of the offender; a crime that necessitates a substantial commitment of resources for a prolonged period of time, or a crime that requires the application of complex or unusual investigative techniques.

Major offenses include:

death investigations	sexual assaults or sex-related felony offenses
robbery investigations	sophisticated burglaries
arsons	organized crime activities
kidnappings	home invasions.

IV. RESPONSIBILITIES FOR CONDUCTING PRELIMINARY INVESTIGATIONS

A. It will be the responsibility of the Patrol Division to conduct preliminary investigations as defined above on all calls for service that involve major offenses.

B. It will be the responsibility of the Patrol Division to conduct preliminary investigations as defined above on all responses to nonmajor offenses.

C. Upon the arrival of the investigator, the patrol officer on the scene shall relinquish responsibility for the investigation, unless otherwise instructed. The responding patrol officer will be responsible for completion of the original offense report, which will include the results of, and actions taken, during the preliminary investigation.

V. RESPONSIBILITIES FOR CONDUCTING FOLLOW-UP INVESTIGATIONS

A. In those cases for which the Patrol Supervisor determines no need for specialized investigative assistance, the Patrol Division will conduct a complete follow-up investigation of the incident.

B. In those cases for which investigative assistance is requested and provided, the investigative division will conduct a comprehensive follow-up investigation of the incident.

C. Follow-up investigation of most misdemeanor crimes can be completed by the Patrol Division. Misdemeanor offenses should be referred to the Investigative Division for follow-up only when the following conditions exist:
   1. The offense appears to be part of a pattern of such offenses.
   2. Follow-up is required in widely separated locations outside the geographic boundaries of the district in which the offense occurred.

D. The Investigative Division will encourage participation by patrol officers in follow-up investigations, when such participation is deemed mutually beneficial by Patrol and Investigative Commanders for the purpose of bringing the case to a speedy and successful conclusion or for enhancement of the professional capabilities of the patrol officer.

APPENDIX 2
INVESTIGATIVE TIME ALLOCATION REPORT

CASE NUMBER: CASE TITLE:
INVESTIGATOR ASSIGNED: DATE ASSIGNED:

INVESTIGATIVE TIME ALLOCATION REPORT

1. The purpose of this form is to capture the investigative time allocated to each case assigned. The Investigative Time Allocation Report will be completed for each case assigned to an investigator. Investigators are responsible for inserting the following information in the appropriate sections of the form:
- Each day a case is worked, an entry regarding time spent on the case will be completed. This entry (or entries) will include the date the activity took place, the amount of time spent on the activity, and a very brief synopsis of the nature of the activity conducted (e.g., interviewed witness, took evidence to the lab, spoke with victim, etc.). This is an *extremely brief summary* of activity that is documented in the investigative report—details are not required on this form.
- The amount of time worked on a case will be reported in 15-minute increments. If more than one detective investigates a case, the total time each detective spends should be totaled and recorded.
2. When the investigator completes the investigation, this form will be attached to the final investigative report and submitted. In the event that additional sheets are needed, as many copies of the "Supplemental Investigative Allocation Report" form shall be utilized, and all copies will be attached to the final investigative report and submitted.

DATE	AMOUNT OF TIME	ACTIVITY
	TOTAL TIME:	

APPENDIX 3
INVESTIGATOR SELECTION PROCESS

Investigator Selection Process

• Announcement to all personnel
• Candidate application
• Investigative scenario
• Candidate interview by a panel of five investigative supervisors

Timetable:
The following timetable should be established for the selection of an officer to the Criminal Investigations Unit:

• Announcement: *(Date when the announcement goes out to all eligible candidates)*
• Application Deadline: *(Allow enough time to advertise and fill out applications)*
• election Deadline: *(Make this date known to eligible candidates)*

The rating process, which is explained in detail below, is proposed to include the following:

• Interview questions
• Investigative scenario
• Application packet
• Professional skills

Application:
The following information should be included in the officer's application for the investigator's position. Attached is a sample application form.

1. Name
2. Law enforcement experience – Police Department and any other experience.
3. Investigative experience – ___ Police Department and any other experience.
4. Investigative training
5. A commentary of the officer's two best investigations while assigned to a patrol function
6. Special skills the officer possesses that would aid him or her in the assignment of an investigator

When the officer submits his or her application, he or she must attach copies of the best investigations cited in the application itself. After the applications are received, two additional cases the applicant has handled on prior occasions will be obtained. These two additional cases may be more indicative of the candidate's *daily* investigative performance. After all of the information is gathered regarding applicants it should be forwarded to the selection committee for their review *prior to* the candidates' interviews.

Interview:
The selection committee will be comprised of _____ investigative supervisors.

The committee will review each candidate's application, and all of the cases attached to the application, with the candidate during his or her interview. In addition, the committee will ask each candidate standardized questions.

When the candidate reports for the interview he or she should initially be given a criminal case scenario to review. The case review will be given first in an effort to induce some stress on the candidate. The candidate should be given 15 minutes to review the case and decide upon a course of action. After the 15 minutes have expired the candidate is called before the committee to review his or her application and answer questions.

After the application review and interview are completed the candidate will be asked to present his or her course of action regarding the criminal case review. Asking the candidate to present his or her case review after the application review and interview should give the selection committee some idea as to how the candidate can function when his or her thought process is interrupted and how well the candidate can think on his or her feet.

The following are some questions that could be asked in the candidate's interview:
1. Why do you want to be an investigator?
2. Explain the daily activities of an investigator in the _____ Police Department.
3. What do you feel should be the criteria for selection of an investigator in the _____ Police Department?
4. What are your strongest attributes that would make you an effective investigator?
5. What skills do you feel you need to improve on to make you a better police officer?

Each of these questions should be rated on a scale of 1 to 3 (1 being the least best answer and 3 being the best answer) by each interviewer. Each interviewer will total his or her ratings and the five ratings will be added together to give a composite rating of the candidate's interview.

The candidate's investigative scenario review presentation should be critiqued based on the following criteria:

1. Thoroughness of review
2. Logical sequence of investigation
3. Knowledge of the law
4. Knowledge of evidentiary value and procedures
5. Creativity
6. Strengths of the case
7. Weaknesses of the case
8. Thoroughness of the proposed investigation.

Each of these criteria should be rated on a scale of 1 to 3 (1 being the least best answer and 3 being the best answer) by each interviewer. Each interviewer will total his or her ratings and the five ratings will be added together to give a composite rating of the case scenario.

In addition to the answers to the previous questions each candidate should be rated by each interviewer on the following criteria that are indicative of *professional* conduct:

1. Punctuality
2. Professional appearance and demeanor
3. Ability to follow directions
4. Verbal communication skills.

Each of these criteria should be rated on a scale of 1 to 3 (1 being the least best answer and 3 being the best answer) by each interviewer. Each interviewer will total his or her ratings and the five ratings will be added together to give a composite rating of the candidate's interview.

After the interview is complete each selection committee member should rate the entire application packet (application and attached case reports) on a scale of 1 to 3 (1 being the least best answer and 3 being the best answer). The interviewers' ratings will be compiled to determine a composite rating for the application packet.

Summary:
A review of the rating process is:

Composite rating of interview questions
Composite rating of criminal case scenario
Composite rating of professional conduct criteria +
Rating of application packet _____
_____

Final rating

APPENDIX 4
INVESTIGATOR APPLICATION

**_____ POLICE DEPARTMENT CRIMINAL
INVESTIGATOR APPLICATION**

Officers interested in applying for the position of investigator with the _____ Police Department must complete this application and submit it to _____ by _____ . Officers must also submit copies of two of the best criminal investigations they have conducted while assigned to the Patrol Division with their application.

NAME:

_____

_____

LAW ENFORCEMENT EXPERIENCE:
_____ **Police Department:** (Include dates and any special assignments)

_____

_____

Other Experience: (Include dates and any special assignments)

_____

_____

_____

_____

_____

_____

_____

INVESTIGATIVE EXPERIENCE:
———————— Police Department: (Include dates and any special assign-ments)

_____

_____

Other Experience: (Include dates and any special assignments)

_____

_____

_____

_____

INVESTIGATIVE TRAINING: (Special training related specifically to investigations)

_____

_____

_____

_____

TWO BEST INVESTIGATIONS WHILE ASSIGNED TO PATROL:

_____

_____

_____

_____

_____

_____

_____

_____

(Include a brief description of each case, including why you feel it is an example of your best work. Include copies of each case with the application.)

_____

_____

_____

_____

_____

_____

_____

_____

_____

_____

_____

_____

_____

_____

_____

_____

_____

_____

_____

_____

_____

_____

_____

_____

SPECIAL SKILLS:
(Include any skills you feel would assist you in your assignment as an investigator with the _____ Police Department.)

_____

_____

_____

_____

_____

_____

_____

_____

_____

_____

_____

_____

_____

_____

_____   _____

Applicant's Signature   Date of Application

APPENDIX 5
INTERVIEW QUESTIONS AND SCORE SHEET

_____ POLICE DEPARTMENT
CRIMINAL INVESTIGATOR INTERVIEW

Candidates are to be rated on each question on a scale of 1 to 3 as follows. When all of the questions are answered the interviewer will total all three ratings at the bottom of the form.

      1 = Below average response
      2 = Average response
      3 = Above average response

QUESTIONS:

1. Why do you want to be an investigator with the _____ Police Department?

Rating: _____

2. Explain the daily activities of an investigator in the _____ Police Department.

Rating: _____

3. What do you feel should be the criteria for selection of an investigator in the _____ Police Department?

Rating: _____

4. What are your strongest attributes that would make you an effective investigator?

Rating: _____

5. What skills do you feel you need to improve on to make you a better police officer?

Rating: _____

TOTAL RATING (Questions): _____

PROFESSIONAL SKILLS

• Punctuality: Rating: _____
  Notes:

• Professional appearance and demeanor: Rating: _____
  Notes:

• Ability to follow directions: Rating: _____
  Notes:

• Verbal communication skills: Rating: _____
  Notes:

TOTAL RATING (Professional skills): _____

INTERVIEWER: _____

APPENDIX 6
CASE SCREENING FORM

_____ **POLICE DEPARTMENT INVESTIGATIONS UNIT**

CASE SCREENING REPORT

Case Report Number: _____ Case Classification: _____

Patrol Officer(s) Assigned: _____ Date: _____

CASE SCREENING
- The Supervisor shall use the following solvability factors to determine which criminal offenses will be investigated.
- The supervisor will circle the applicable solvability factors and then add the factors to obtain a total weight regarding the possibility of solving a crime.
- f the total weight of the solvability factors equals 10 or more, the case shall be assigned to an investigator for further investigation.

SOLVABILITY FACTOR   **SOLVABILITY WEIGHT**

1. Estimated time lapse of crime discovery
   a. Less than 1 hour   3
   b. 1-12 hours   2
   c. 12-24 hours   1
   d. More than 24 hours   0
2. Crime discovered on-view by officer   5
3. Witness to crime (weight depends on credibility)   1 2 3 4 5
4. Suspect can be identified   10
5. Suspect can be described   4
6. Suspect can be located   4
7. Suspect has been seen in the area previous
   to the offense   2
8. Suspect vehicle can be identified   7
9. Suspect vehicle can be partially described 2
10. Stolen property can be traced   5
11. Stolen property has been recovered   7

SOLVABILITY FACTOR   SOLVABILITY WEIGHT

Solvability Factor	Solvability Weight
12. Significant/unique method of operation	3
13. Significant amount of physical evidence recovered	3
14. Recovered latent fingerprints	5
15. Limited opportunity for offender to commit the crime	4
16. Other consideration/impact on the community	1 2 3 4 5

TOTAL: _____

APPENDIX 7
VICTIM FOLLOW-UP LETTER (CASE ASSIGNED)

YOUR DEPARTMENT NAME HERE

Date

Name of Crime Victim

Dear Mr./Mrs./Ms. _____
On (date police were notified) you notified the _____ Police Department of a (fill in blank with type of crime that occurred). This incident has been assigned Case Report # _____.

Please review the attached report that was completed regarding the incident to make certain that it is complete.

In the event that you have additional information that could assist us in this investigation, or if any information has been omitted from the report, please contact the investigator assigned to your investigation, Investigator _____ at _____

Thank you for your cooperation.

Sincerely,

APPENDIX 8
VICTIM FOLLOW-UP LETTER
(NO CASE ASSIGNED)

YOUR DEPARTMENT NAME HERE

Date

Name of Crime Victim

Dear Mr./Mrs./Ms. _____

On (date police were notified) you notified the _____ Police Department of a (fill in blank with type of crime that occurred). This incident has been assigned Case Report # _____

Unfortunately, as of this date no new leads or information have come to the attention of the _____ Police Department that would allow us to further investigate this matter.

Please review the attached report that was completed regarding the incident to make certain that it is complete.

In the event that you have additional information that could assist us in this investigation, or if any information has been omitted from the report, please contact _____ at _____

Thank you for your cooperation.

Sincerely,

APPENDIX 9
INVESTIGATIVE SUMMARY REPORT

INVESTIGATIVE SUMMARY REPORT

CASE NAME: _____ CASE NUMBER: _____

INVESTIGATOR ASSIGNED: _____

DATE OPENED: _____

SYNOPSIS:
This includes a brief synopsis of the case, enough to provide the reader with a basic understanding of the offense and facts surrounding the incident.

CHAIN OF CUSTODY OF EVIDENTIARY ITEMS:
The date that the evidentiary items were recovered, the recovering officer, and the current location should be listed in chronological order.

DEFENDANTS CRIMINAL HISTORY:

LIST OF WITNESSES:

TABLE OF CONTENTS:
All reports should be placed in chronological order and numbered. The list of page numbers and a brief description of the report is listed here.

APPENDIX 10
INVESTIGATIVE PLAN

_____ POLICE DEPARTMENT

INVESTIGATIVE PLAN

Instructions: Following review of the incident report, decide what investigative steps you feel are appropriate for this follow-up investigation. List the steps in chronological order, numbering each step in the order in which you feel it should be completed. Insert a short narrative of the planned activity and an estimated completion date. Keep in mind that the investigative process is by nature a fluid and flexible process, and the order in which these activities are conducted may change as new leads are developed.

When the form is completed, please return it to _____ for review and discussion with you.

Incident Number: _____ Date of Incident: _____

Investigator Assigned: _____

Number	Activity to be Conducted	Est. Completion Date

APPENDIX 11
CASE REVIEW FORM

YOUR DEPARTMENT NAME HERE

CASE REVIEW

Case Title: _____ Case Number:_____

Investigator Assigned:_____ Date Opened: _____

Date of Review	Comments	Pending/ Closed Date	Date of Next Review

APPENDIX 12
COMPUTERIZED CASE REVIEW FORM

CASE REVIEW

Case Number:　　　　　　　　　　　　Investigator Assigned:

Date Opened:

Date of Review:

Comments:

Date of Next Review:

Date of Review:

Comments:

Date of Next Review:

Date of Review:

Comments:

Date of Next Review:

Date of Review:

Comments:

Date of Next Review:

Date of Review:

Comments:

Date of Next Review:

APPENDIX 13
C/S REFERRAL CARD

(FRONT)   (BACK)

CONFIDENTIAL SOURCE

REFERRAL CARD

NAME: _____

AKA:

ADDRESS: _____

DOB: _____
SSAN: _____
DL#: _____
HT: ____ WT: ____ SEX: ____
RACE: _____
HOME PHONE: _____
WORK PHONE: _____
PAGER/CELL: _____

CURRENT CHARGES:
_____
_____

PREVIOUS CRIM. HISTORY:
_____
_____

GANG AFFILIATION: _____

RETURN THIS FORM TO THE
INVESTIGATIONS UNIT WITH
A COPY OF YOUR FIELD
REPORT OR CITATION(S)
ATTACHED

INFORM ARRESTEE: IT IS POSSIBLE TO RECEIVE LENIENCY OR CONSIDERATION ON CURRENT CHARGES IF HE OR SHE CAN PROVIDE INFORMATION REGARDING OTHER CRIMES OR OTHER PERSONS INVOLVED IN CRIMINAL ACTIVITY. NO EXPLICIT OR IMPLICIT PROMISES CAN BE MADE REGARDING DISPOSITION OF PENDING CHARGES, BUT HIS OR HER COOPERATION WILL BE MADE KNOWN TO PROSECUTORS.

THERE IS ALSO A POTENTIAL FOR CASH PAYMENTS FOR INFORMATION OR INTRODUCTIONS TO SUSPECTS.

POTENTIAL INFORMATION:
NARCOTICS:_____
PROPERTY CRIMES: _____
VIOLENT CRIMES: _____
ORGANIZED CRIME: _____
OTHER CRIME: _____

APPENDIX 14
C/S REGISTRATION FORM

_____ **POLICE DEPARTMENT**
CONFIDENTIAL SOURCE REGISTRATION FORM

C/S NAME: _____ TRUE NAME: _____

RACE/SEX/DOB: _____ CITY OF RESIDENCE: _____

CONFIDENTIAL SOURCE ADVISEMENT
(HAVE THE C/S READ CAREFULLY, INITIAL EACH POINT
AND SIGN BELOW)

I understand that while I am acting as a Confidential Source (C/S) for the _____ Police Department, I am forbidden to do any of the following:

1. Sell or deliver any Controlled Substance, or any substance purported to be a controlled substance to anyone.
2. Use sex or sexual activity to induce the sale or delivery of any controlled substance or the commission of any criminal act.
3. Search any person, vehicle, or structure.
4. Become involved in any activity that could be construed as entrapment. Those acts that constitute entrapment have been clearly explained to me, and I fully understand what constitutes entrapment.
5. Engage in any illegal activity or improper conduct as long as I am working as a C/S, to include carrying a weapon or impersonating a police officer.
6. I understand that if violations of the law can be substantiated against me, I will be prosecuted.
7. I am agreeing to function as a C/S of my own free will, and not as the result of any intimidation, promises, or threats.
8. I understand that any payments made to me are considered taxable income for tax filing.
9. I understand that no police officer may make any explicit or implicit promises or predictions regarding the likely disposition of any criminal charges pending against me, only that my cooperation will be made known to the prosecuting authorities.

C/S Signature: _____ True Signature: _____
C/S Name Printed:_____ True Name Printed: _____
Witness: _____ Date: _____ Time: _____

APPENDIX 15
C/S FUND AND PAYMENT POLICY

_____ POLICE DEPARTMENT
CONFIDENTIAL SOURCE REGISTRATION POLICY

INTRODUCTION

Confidential Sources (C/S) can provide information on crimes about to occur, introductions of undercover officers to persons engaged in criminal activities, and information on crimes that have already occurred. Many crimes could not be solved without information having been provided concerning the perpetrators, and in those instances, the value of confidential informants is most evident.

PURPOSE

In order to enhance law enforcement efforts and maintain safety of officers utilizing Confidential Sources, it is necessary to establish a policy for their use.

POLICY

It is the policy of the Police Department to register any Confidential Source who is to be provided payment for information and/or services.

PROCEDURE

Opening of Confidential Source files:
When an officer desires to utilize an individual as a Confidential Source, the officer must complete the following:

1. Confidential Source Advisement and Registration Form
2. Fingerprinting

3. Photographing
4. Personal History Form.

The confidential source will then be provided with a fictitious name and Confidential Source registration number. The number shall consist of the date in numbers, followed by a 2-digit number specifically assigned to the confidential informant. In the event that more than one Confidential Sources are registered on the same day, the 2-digit number will be increased by one. (Example: the first confidential source registered on October 18, 2003, would be assigned the number "10180301," the second "10180302," etc.)

This fictitious name and registration number will be utilized on all receipts for official funds, and can be used in reports when using the Confidential Source's actual or fictitious name would not be appropriate. The registration information will be placed into the Confidential Source's file, as will any receipts for official funds.

SECURITY OF CONFIDENTIAL SOURCE FILES

The information contained in confidential source files, if compromised, could lead to situations in which the safety of the Confidential Source, undercover police officers, and police operations could be negatively impacted. It is therefore imperative that the appropriate level of security over the C/S files be maintained. It is the responsibility of the Chief of Police or his designee to maintain security of the confidential source files.

CLOSING CONFIDENTIAL SOURCE FILES

In the event that a C/S permanently leaves the area or otherwise renders himself or herself unable to provide further information, the C/S file will be closed and securely maintained by the Chief of Police or his designee. This file will be maintained for a period of 5 years from the date of closing.

_____ **POLICE DEPARTMENT**
CONFIDENTIAL SOURCE OFFICIAL FUND POLICY

INTRODUCTION

The use of Confidential Sources to uncover various types of criminal activity can involve situations in which the Confidential Sources are paid for their services. In addition to payment of Confidential Sources for services rendered, it is often necessary for undercover officers to make controlled purchases of contraband utilizing Confidential Sources, or to utilize money to make undercover purchases of contraband themselves.

The funds utilized to make these payments/purchases come from three main sources:

1. Money that has been seized in controlled substance investigations and has been awarded to the department by a court through an Asset Forfeiture Proceeding.
2. Money that has been donated by outside sources and specifically designated for the aforementioned purposes.
3. Money allocated for these purposes as part of the police department budget.

PURPOSE

In order to maintain fiscal responsibility and the integrity of a compensation program for Confidential Sources, it is necessary to establish a program for the administration and operation of the program.
The policy established must address accounting practices to be utilized, methods of payment, reporting procedures, and responsibility for auditing and review of the program. This policy must eliminate, as much as possible, the potential for abuse.

POLICY

It is the policy of the _____ Police Department to maintain a fund for investigative purposes. The money contained in the fund may be utilized for the following purposes:

a. Purchase of evidence, to include narcotics, stolen property, and/or other contraband by undercover police officers and/or Confidential Sources.
b. Payment of Confidential Sources for information provided regarding criminal activity.
c. Payment for extraordinary expenses incurred during investigations.

AUTHORITY

The authority over the fund shall rest with the Chief of Police or his designee, who must approve any and all expenditures from the Confidential Source Official Fund by department personnel.

ACCOUNTING

Any officer using funds will complete a Monthly Statement, which accounts for all funds received, transferred, or expended. Receipts for transferred funds, expenditures made, and purchases made will be attached.
In addition, the Chief of Police or his designee will complete a monthly report reflecting the beginning and ending monthly balance and total expenditures for the fund.
The Chief of Police will also prepare a yearly statement for presentation to the, and will cooperate with any audits deemed appropriate by the _____.

PROCEDURES

When an officer wishes to utilize funds for purposes outlined under POLICY, approval must be sought from the Chief of Police or his designee.

a. Receipt of Funds:
The Chief of Police or his designee will prepare a check, made out to the officer, who will complete a Receipt of Investigative Funds form. The officer will sign the form in the space provided for Witness, and will maintain a copy of the receipt for inclusion in his or her monthly statement. The Chief of Police or his designee will maintain the original for inclusion in his or her monthly statement.
The officer will then cash the check and utilize the funds for the purpose(s) approved at the time of issuance.

b. Redeposit of Funds:

In the event that the money is not utilized, or at the direction of the Chief of Police or his designee, the officer will redeposit the money into the Confidential Source Official Fund account. The officer will retain the deposit slip for his or her monthly statement.

c. Use of Funds:

1. Confidential Informant Payment: When an officer makes an approved payment of funds to a registered Confidential Source, he or she will complete a Receipt/Expenditure of Investigative Funds form, and have the

Confidential Source sign the form with the fictitious name and the Confidential Source number. This receipt will be included in the officer's monthly statement. Attached to the form will be a copy of the police report or a memorandum detailing the purpose for the expenditure and the case number.

2. Purchase of Evidence: When an officer makes a purchase of evidence, whether it is an undercover purchase by the officer, or a controlled purchase by a Confidential Source, a police report or a memorandum detailing the purpose for the expenditure and the case number will be attached to the officer's monthly statement.

3. Extraordinary Investigative Expenditure: When an officer expends funds for investigative purposes, a memorandum detailing the purpose for the expenditure and the case number will be attached to the officer's monthly statement, along with receipts (if available) from the expenditure.

_____ **POLICE DEPARTMENT**
RECEIPT/EXPENDITURE OF INVESTIGATIVE FUNDS

Purpose: Purchase of Evidence ( ) Information and Services ( ) Protection Expenses ( )

Case Number: _____

I hereby acknowledge the receipt of funds in the amount of _____and   /100 dollars ($_____),

provided to me by _____.

Provided by: _____ Date: _____

Witnessed by: _____ Date: _____

Confidential Source Signature: _____

Date: _____

Confidential Source Number: _____

_____POLICE DEPARTMENT
MONTHLY STATEMENT FOR INVESTIGATIVE FUNDS

Officer Name and ID: _____

Reporting Period: _____

Balance on Hand Beginning of Period: _____

Advances Received: Amount: _____ Date: _____

Amount: _____ Date: _____

Amount: _____ Date: _____

Total to Be Accounted For: _____

Total Expended: _____

Expenditures: Case Number _____ Amount _____

Expenditures: Case Number _____ Amount _____

Expenditures: Case Number _____ Amount _____

Balance on Hand at End of Period: _____

This is to certify that the transactions recorded hereon are complete and accurate, and that the expenditures have been made for official purposes as part of the cases referenced.

Signature of Office _____ Date _____

This is to certify that I have counted the reporting officer's cash on hand and it is the same as Balance on Hand at End of Period.

Signature of Supervisor _____ Date _____

APPENDIX 16
OPERATIONAL PLAN

_____ **POLICE DEPARTMENT**
OPERATIONAL PLAN

CASE #:   CASE TITLE: CASE CASE
                                          OFFICER:

DATE:_____ TIME: SUPERVISOR:

TYPE OF ACTIVITY: ☐ BUY/BUST ☐ SEARCH

WARRANT ☐ REVERSE ARREST ☐ OTHER

DESCRIPTION: _____

LOCATION: _____ MEET LOCATION: _____

MAJOR STREETS: _____

NEAREST HOSPITAL: _____ MAJOR STREETS: _____

EMERGENCY MEDICAL EVACUATION (HELICOPTER) PHONE # ____

NEAREST POLICE DEPARTMENT: _____ PHONE # _____

U/C AGENT: _____ U/C VEHICLE: _____ MONEY ___ PERSON: _____

BLOOD TYPE _____ BLOOD TYPE _____

CI WITH U/C nYES n NO CI # _____ ATTIRE _____

CI DESCRIPTION: SEX ____ RACE ____ HAIR ____ HT. ____ WT. _____

ARREST SIGNAL: _____ BACK UP SIGNAL: _____

DEFENDANTS/SUSPECTS:

NAME:	SEX/RACE	AGE	HT.	WT.	HAIR	ADDRESS	CAUTION

SUSPECTED CONNECT: _____ ADDRESS:_____

SUSPECTED VEHICLES:

YEAR AND MAKE	MODEL	COLOR	LICENSE	REGISTERED OWNER

ASSISTING OUTSIDE AGENCIES: ___ PROCESSING LOCATION: ___

MAP OF BUY/BUST OR ARREST AREA

SYNOPSIS OF BUY/BUST OR ARREST

BRIEF HISTORY OF CASE

APPENDIX 17
ROOM CONFIGURATION-EVALUATION DESIGN

Screen

Laptop and Projector

INDEX